Practical Phonology

Practical Phonology

Dorothea Bogle

Moray House
Publications
1996

Published by Moray House Institute of Education
Holyrood Road, Edinburgh

First published 1996

ISBN 0 901580 562

©1996 Dorothea Bogle

Printed and bound in Great Britain by
BPC–AUP Aberdeen Ltd

CONTENTS

Preface

THIS TEXT PROVIDES an introduction to the sound system of English. Although it was originally intended for teachers of English as a Foreign Language at home and overseas, it will provide useful insights for all students of linguistics and those interested in speech.

It consists of four complementary sections. The first two deal with phonological theory and establish a basis for description. The third section consists of a workbook in phonemic transcription and is intended for ongoing practice to supplement parts 1 and 2. The last section contains suggestions for activities which will help young learners to develop receptive and productive pronunciation skills as a meaningful and integrated part of classroom practice.

Although learners usually rank the acquisition of a 'good' spoken model as a high priority, teachers have tended to regard phonology as a difficult and technical study. It is important to demonstrate that the theory can be made accessible and that it has relevance for classroom practice within the current approach to language teaching.

The impetus to compile the present text was a requirement to write distance-learning materials on phonology and the teaching of pronunciation for master's level students at home and overseas. Restrictions on space and time allocation in SEH (student effort hours) meant that only a small proportion of the subject could be covered in detail. I felt the need for additional backup materials which would allow course members the possibility to progress at a more leisurely pace. Although many would already have covered some course in phonology, it could not be assumed that all students would have a background in this area. This book therefore aims to establish a basic, user-friendly introduction to the sound system of English. There is no intention to examine current theoretical issues. These have been addressed by other writers. The present workbook assumes no prior knowledge, and provides many applicational tasks to encourage learners to build up their expertise over a period. The approach is essentially practice-focused with a theoretical concept being immediately linked to tasks which will allow students to check their understanding. Answers are supplied at the back of each part in the traditional form.

The book is based on many years of experience in teaching phonology to generations of students – undergraduates, postgraduates and teacher-trainers. The approach was developed by a team of phoneticians working in the Speech Unit at Moray House Institute of Education, and I would like to thank my former colleagues for their help and guidance. It has always been our belief that phonology could and should be an interesting and practical subject in the curriculum and one which has a great deal to offer the enthusiastic learner. We would all like to pay special tribute to the late Professor David Abercrombie of the Department of Phonetics, University of Edinburgh, who was a mentor and inspiration to all his students.

PART ONE:
A Framework
for Description

PHONOLOGY, grammar and vocabulary describe the systems of the language. Phonology examines the sound-system. Each language selects a collection of meaningful sounds (or phonemes) from the vast reservoir of possible human speech sounds and uses them to form distinctive contrasts in that language. For example, English differentiates between 'r' and 'l' in words like 'right' and 'light', and 'a' and 'u' in 'cat' and 'cut'. The sounds 'r' and 'l' and 'a' and 'u' therefore function as separate phonemes in English, although they do not have phonemic status in Japanese for example. In addition to the phonemes, the basic building blocks, each language may group the sounds differently to form the syllable-structure. English allows 'str-' at the beginning of a word (string, straw) but 'stl-' is not a possibility. Knowledge of the phonology of the language includes not only an awareness of which sounds are acceptable and how they may co-occur, but also an understanding of which patterns are not permissible as part of the system.

Clearly, all languages function at a level above the single word and it is essential to tune in to meaningful features of connected speech both as a listener and as a speaker. As soon as two or more syllables occur together, the phenomenon of stress becomes important since one syllable in the stream of speech stands out more than the others which become weakened by contrast. Since word stress is a major clue to correct word identification, this is a phonological feature which needs to be taken into account from an early stage in vocabulary-building.

The regular occurence of the stress, or the beat, in connected text builds up to the rhythm of the language. The stresses in English tend to fall on the important information-carrying items in the language, with the low-information words becoming backgrounded by contrast:

This is the **first** of **May**

The main focus of the message can be altered significantly in order to enable the listener to make the correct interpretation of the meaning:

<u>**This**</u> is the **first** of **May**
(today, not tomorrow)

This is the <u>**first**</u> of **May**
(not the second)

This is the **first** of <u>**May**</u>
(neutral / not June)

Another of the tools which the speaker uses to accompany the vocabulary and grammar is appropriate choice of intonation patterns. These can convey both grammatical contrasts ('Yes?'↗ vs 'Yes'↘) and attitudinal features ('Well' 😕 = doubtful or 'Of course!' 🙂 = enthusiasm). This is a difficult area to describe even for native speakers and needs recognition skills to be built up gradually.

It is important for teachers to have a clear framework for description of the phonological system so that they are aware of how the sound-patterns carry contrastive information in the language. This will heighten their awareness of their own spoken model if they are non-native speakers, and will provide a basis against which to identify particular features of phonological difficulty. It will also suggest remedies to enable learners to operate the sound system more accurately.

Building from the smallest unit to the largest, the phonological hierarchy consists of:

The phoneme   /p/   p
The syllable   /penz/   pens
The rhythm unit   /penz ər ɪn ðə/ pens are in the
The intonation unit //penz ər ɪn ðə /kʌbəd //
                   pens are in the cupboard

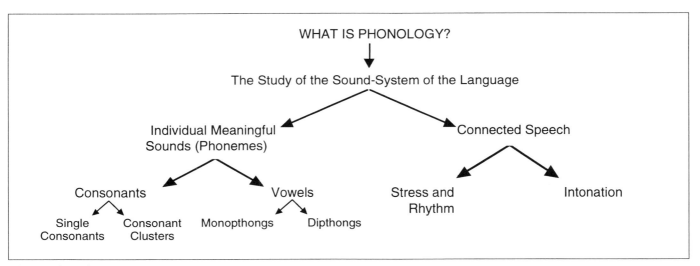

Fig. 1: Phonology

Which English?

Before embarking upon a detailed description of the phonological features mentioned above, it is important to specify which accent of English is to be described. Learners of English will be aware of a variety of different regional accents, all of which are equally legitimate as the appropriate means of communication in their own context (Indian English in India, General American in the U.S.A., East African English in Kenya, and Cockney English in the London area). This variety in possible models can give rise to some concern and confusion for learners. However, for teaching purposes, it is customary to target an internationally intelligible model as a framework for description, not because it is in any way better than any other accent but simply because it is understood without difficulty by all educated speakers of the language. In addition, most dictionaries and course books will describe this framework accent. For present purposes therefore, it is useful to follow the example of others and use the internationally intelligible model known as Received Pronunciation (R.P.) or as B.B.C. English as the starting point against which to compare other spoken models, with the proviso that we are describing – and not prescribing – this accent (or way of pronouncing) as the reference model.

As teachers, it is interesting to build up our awareness of how our own spoken models compare and contrast with this accent. The number of native speakers of English who actually speak R.P. is surprisingly small and it would be an unrealistic (and undesirable) goal for all learners of English to aim to speak R.P., despite the expectations of a number of over-enthusiastic students! Good communication and a comfortably intelligible model are realistic and achievable expectations and should be encouraged.

If the goal is good communication – transfer of the message with no breakdown due to the spoken realisations – which are the features to be mastered?

This is best answered by starting with a description of how speech is produced since this will help to explain some of the categories required for description.

Phonemes

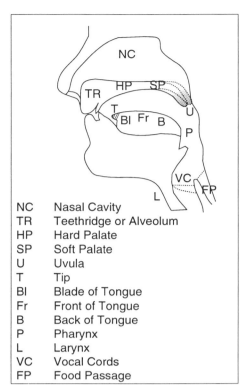

NC	Nasal Cavity
TR	Teethridge or Alveolum
HP	Hard Palate
SP	Soft Palate
U	Uvula
T	Tip
Bl	Blade of Tongue
Fr	Front of Tongue
B	Back of Tongue
P	Pharynx
L	Larynx
VC	Vocal Cords
FP	Food Passage

Fig. 2: The Vocal Tract

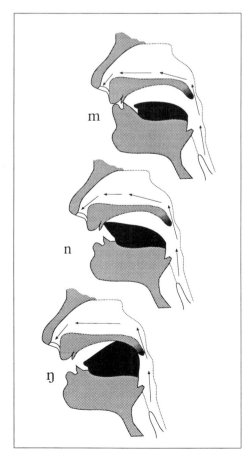

Fig. 3: Nasals: / ŋ / is the sound which is spelt as '–ng', as in 'sing'.

How Speech Sounds are Produced

In order for sound to be produced there must be movement of air. In this case, the movement is produced by the airstream mechanism which is expelled from the lungs and pushed up the passage known as the vocal tract towards the mouth and outer air.

Voicing

As the airstream enters the larynx, it encounters a pair of muscular lips, joined at the front and free-flowing at the back in the shape of a 'v'. If these muscles, or vocal cords, are apart the air moves on up the vocal tract without interference and the resulting sound is labelled as voiceless. If on the other hand the vocal cords are vibrating, the sound produced is voiced. The tongue, teeth and lips remain in the same position. The only change is in the action of the vocal cords.
For example:

Voiceless sounds (-v)	*Voiced sounds* (+v)
s	z
f	v

Put your hand on your throat and move from 's' to 'z'

$$ssss - zzzz - ssss - zzzz$$

You should feel the vibration in the throat caused by rapid movements of the vocal cords for the voiced sound 'z'.

Oral and Nasal Sounds

The airstream moves further up the vocal tract until it reaches the soft palate. If you curl your tongue backwards along the hard boney ridge over the roof of your mouth, you will reach the soft section at the back. This area is called the soft palate (or velum). If the soft palate is lowered, the airstream is channelled up and through the nose (via the nasal cavity). Sounds produced with this nasal escape are called the nasals; an example of a nasal in English is 'm' illustrated in Figure 3.

If the soft palate is raised, the airstream flows in to the mouth, and the sounds produced are called oral. Close your lips together and make the sound 'p'. This is a sound produced at the lips (labial) with the airstream completely closed or stopped; therefore it belongs to the category of phonemes called stops. 'p' is a labial stop produced with the vocal cords apart, therefore it is described as a voiceless labial stop. 'b' is produced in the same place, except that the vocal cords are vibrating so it is known as a voiced labial stop (see Figure 4). 'm' is again produced with a closure at the lips, but the airstream escapes through the nose, so it is called a labial nasal.

Stops

The airstream may be stopped at different places in the mouth, at different "places of articulation". 'p' and 'b' are stopped at the lips with a closure between the upper and lower lip.

't' and 'd' are stopped behind the upper teeth with a closure produced by the blade of the tongue and the tooth-ridge, or alveolum (see Figure 4).

'k' and 'g' are stopped at the back of the mouth with a closure between the back of the tongue and the soft palate (see Figure 4).

We have seen how /p/, /b/ and /m/ group together as they are all produced at the same place of articulation. Similarly, we can build up families of sounds behind the upper teeth (alveolum) and at the soft palate (velum).

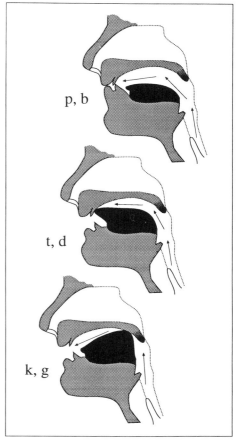

p, b

t, d

k, g

Fig. 4: Stops

PLACE → MANNER ↓	Lips (labial)		Teeth (alveolar)		Soft Palate (velar)	
	− v	+ v	− v	+ v	− v	+ v
stop	p	b	t	d	k	g
nasal	−	m	−	n	−	ŋ

Fig. 5

Now do exercises 1 and 2

We are now in a position to describe the consonants of English as we have already encountered the three important features necessary for identification:

Voicing	whether the vocal cords are apart or vibrating (voiceless [-v] or voiced [+v])
Place of articulation	where the sounds are produced, and which articulators (parts of the vocal tract) are involved, e.g. labial, velar.
Manner of articulation	how the sounds are produced in terms of how the airstream is restricted on its passage up the vocal tract, e.g. stop, nasal.

The Consonants of English

Consonants in languages are described with reference to the three-term label:

> Voiced or voiceless
> Place of articulation
> Manner of articulation

The basic distinction between consonants and vowels is that the consonants are produced with a degree of restriction of the airstream at some point along the vocal tract, whereas the vowels are produced with only minimal restriction, technically termed *open approximation*.

Place of Articulation

This describes the place where the airstream is restricted on a front to back axis.

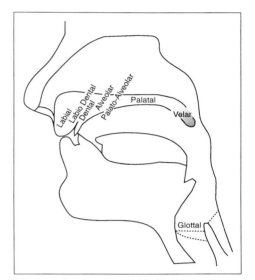

Fig. 6: Places of Articulation

Place	*Articulators*	*Phonemes*
Labial:	the lips	/p/, /b/, /m/, /w/
Labio-dental:	upper teeth, lower lip	/f/, /v/
Dental:	tongue tip between the upper and lower teeth	/θ/, /ð/
Alveolar:	blade of tongue, teethridge	/s/, /z/, /t/, /d/
Palato-alveolar:	blade of tongue in contact with area between teethridge and hard palate	/ʃ/, /ʒ/, /tʃ/, /dʒ/
Palatal:	front of tongue, hard palate	/j/
Velar:	back of tongue, soft palate	/k/, /g/, /ŋ/

Manner of Articulation

This refers to the way in which the airstream escapes into the outer air.

Stop: the airstream is momentarily stopped (/p/ /b/, /t/ /d/, /k/ /g).

Nasal: the airstream escapes through the nose (/m/, /n/, /ŋ/).

Lateral: the airstream passes over the sides of the tongue since there is a closure between the blade and teethridge (/l/).

Affricate: the airstream is stopped then released with a fricative off-glide (/tʃ/, /dʒ/).

Fricative: the airstream squeezes through a narrow opening between the articulators and causes friction (/f/, /s/, /ʃ/, /θ/)

Approximant: the tongue moves up towards the upper articulator but not close enough to produce friction i.e. it approximates to the upper articulator (/w/, /r/, /j/).

It is not envisaged that learners should be able to refer to these technical terms as expertly as phoneticians, but it is nevertheless important to understand the processes involved and to recognise the labels if they are referred to elsewhere. It is usually enough for example to be aware that /θ/ and /t/ are different both in place of articulation (dental vs alveolar) and in manner of articulation (fricative vs stop). Whereas the phonetician would describe /θ/ as a voiceless dental fricative, the classroom teacher might simply ask learners to 'put their tongues between their teeth and blow'.

Those anxious to pursue their expertise in this area may wish to complete the list below, using the chart of the consonants of English in on the next page as a guideline.

To help you practise using the phonetic symbols like /θ/ and /ʃ/, turn to Part 3 and work through Tasks 1–5.

Consonants of English (R.P.)

		word-initial c –	word-final – c	medial – c –
1	/ p /	pin	sip	happy
2	/ b /	bin	mob	hobby
3	/ t /	ten	net	better
4	/ d /	done	nod	body
5	/ k /	come	luck	shaking
6	/ g /	gun	hug	beggar
7	/ m /	man	ham	hammer
8	/ n /	nut	run	runner
9	/ ŋ /	-	sing	singer
10	/ f /	fat	rough	safer
11	/ v /	very	leave	ever
12	/ θ /	thin	cloth	nothing
13	/ ð /	then	loathe	clothing
14	/ s /	see	piece	looser
15	/ z /	zoo	bees	loser
16	/ ʃ /	ship	rush	pusher
17	/ ʒ /	-	rouge	measure
18	/ tʃ /	chip	catch	itchy
19	/ dʒ /	jam	edge	edging
20	/ w /	win	-	away
21	/ l /	let	tell	sailing
22	/ r /	run	-	hurry
23	/ j /	you	-	beyond
24	/ h /	he	-	ahead

Description

	Keyword	Voicing	Place	Manner
/p/	pen	voiceless	labial	stop
/b/	baby	voiced	labial	stop
/t/	tap	voiceless	alveolar	stop
/d/	dog	voiced	alveolar	stop
/k/	cat	voiceless	velar	stop
/g/	goat	voiced	velar	stop
/m/	mouse	voiced	labial	nasal
/n/	nurse	voiced	alveolar	
/ŋ/	king	voiced		
/θ/	thief			
/ð/	feather			
/f/	fish			
/v/	van			
/s/	sun			
/z/	zebra			
/ʒ/	treasure			
/tʃ/	church			
/dʒ/	giant			
/l/	lion			
/r/	rabbit			
/j/	yacht			
/w/	witch			
/h/	hen			

Place→ Manner ↓	Labial	Labio- Dental	Dental	Alveolar	Palato- Alveolar	Palatal	Velar	Glottal
stop	/p/ /b/			/t/ /d/			/k/ /g/	
nasal	/m/			/n/			/ŋ/	
lateral				/l/				
affricate					/tʃ/ /dʒ/			
fricative		/f/ /v/	/θ/ /ð/	/s/ /z/	/ʃ/ /ʒ/			/h/
approximant	/w/			/r/		/j/		

Fig. 7: Chart of the consonants used in English (R.P.), showing degree of voicing, place and manner of articulation. Notice that the symbols for voiceless sounds are always placed on the left side of the pigeon hole and voiced sounds on the right.

Consonant Clusters and Syllable Structure

A consonant cluster is a group of two or more consonants which occur together without any intervening vowel. They may occur word-initially as in 'clouds' /kl-/ or word-finally 'clouds' /-dz/. English has a complex system of clusters and this causes considerable problems for people whose mother tongues do not allow similar 'syllable-structure' patterns. The result is that clusters are broken up with intrusive vowels ('eschool' or 'sepoon') or even omitted altogether so that 'jump', 'jumps', and 'jumped' are all pronounced identically with the resultant grammatical breakdowns.

Syllable Structure

A typical monosyllabic word in English has a simple pattern such as:

Consonant (c)	Vowel (v)	Consonant (c)
c	a	p
r	u	n
f	ee	l

However, it is also possible to have other patterns such as:

	Vowel	Consonant
eel	ee	l

or

	Consonant	Vowel
fee	f	ee

The syllable structure of the following one-syllable words would be:

march	C	V	C	/ mɑːtʃ /
art	-	V	C	/ ɑːt /
large	C	V	C	/ lɑːdʒ /
car	C	V	-	/ kɑː /

Remember that:

- / r / is not pronounced syllable-finally in R.P.
- 'sh', 'th', and 'ch' count as one phoneme each (= C)
- Although they are spelt with two letters, diphthongs and long vowels also count as *one* phoneme (= V).

Now do Exercise 3.

Exercise 3

Write down the syllable structure for the following monosyllablic words:

ship	they	charge	all	fur

Word Initial Consonant Clusters

English allows groups of two or three consonants at the beginning of a syllable.

Two consonants: (CC VC)

	C	C	V	C	
proud	p	r	ou	d	/ praʊd /
smoke	s	m	o	ke	/ sməʊk /
black	b	l	a	ck	/ blæk /
fright	f	r	i	ght	/ fraɪt /
news	n	j	ew	s	/ njuːz /

Three Consonants   (CCC VC)

	C	C	C	V	C	
spring	s	p	r	i	ng	/ sprɪŋ /
splash	s	p	l	a	sh	/ splæʃ /
stream	s	t	r	ea	m	/ striːm /
scratch	s	c	r	a	tch	/ skrætʃ /
squares	s	k w (qu)		are	s	/ skweəz/

Now do Exercise 4.

Exercise 4

Write down the syllable structure for the following words. Remember that we are concerned with *sounds* not letters

e.g. 'clouds' = CCVCC

school	crash	string	stew	shrewd	pure

Notice that where three consonants occur in an initial cluster, the first consonant is always /s/:

s	p	r	ing
s	c	r	atch
s	t	r	ap

$C_1 = /s/$

The second consonant is:

/ p, t, k / $\qquad$ $C_2 = /p, t, k/$

The third consonant is:

/ r, l / or / w, j / $\qquad$ $C_3 = / r, l, w, j /$

However, phonemes cluster only in certain combinations so that /spl-/ is possible in English but /stl-/ is not permissible. Knowledge of phonology will indicate which groups are acceptable and also those which are impossible within the set.

Word Final Consonant Clusters

In the syllable-final position, the permissible clustering of consonants is more complex and more important because they carry information about grammatical distinctions such as possessives, plurals and tenses.

Two consonants: (– CC)

	C	C	V	C	C	
hens		h	e	n	s	/ henz /
stand	s	t	a	n	d	/ stænd /
washed		w	a	sh	ed	/ wɒʃt /
climbed	c	l	i	mb	ed	/ klaɪmd /
walks		w	al	k	s	/ wɔːks /

You should particularly notice the use of {–s} in plurals, possessives, third person singular (ha<u>ts</u>, cat'<u>s</u>, she si<u>ts</u>). There is a *consonant-harmony* in operation here whereby a voiceless root will take a voiceless ending /– s/:

duck	duck + s	/ dʌks /
cat	cat + s	/ kæts /

whereas a voiced root will take /-z/

dog	dog + z	/ dɒgz /
lamb	lamb + z	/ læmz /

If the root form finishes in a 'sibilant' (/s/, /z/, /tʒ/, /ʃ/, /dʒ/) the plural will be formed with / –ɪz /.

fox	fox + /ɪz/	/fɒksɪz/
watch	watch + /ɪz/	/wɒtʃɪz/

Now do Exercise 5.

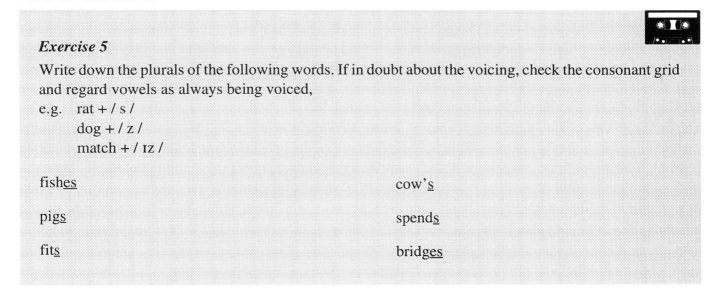

Exercise 5

Write down the plurals of the following words. If in doubt about the voicing, check the consonant grid and regard vowels as always being voiced,

e.g.   rat + / s /
        dog + / z /
        match + / ɪz /

fishe<u>s</u>   cow'<u>s</u>

pig<u>s</u>   spend<u>s</u>

fit<u>s</u>   brid<u>ges</u>

{-ed}: the same phonological rule operates for the past tense of weak verbs so that a voiceless root form will add / t / in the past tense ('watched' / wɒtʃt /), a voiced root will add /d/ ('gazed' / geɪzd) and a root ending in / t / or / d / will add / ɪd / ('painted' / peɪntɪd / and 'nodded' /nɒdɪd/).

Now do Exercise 6.

Exercise 6

Write down the {-ed} endings for the following examples,

e.g.   talk   talked /+t /
        climb   climbed /+d /
        add   added /+ ɪd /

                                    plant<u>ed</u>
liv<u>ed</u>
                                    brush<u>ed</u>
rush<u>ed</u>
                                    burn<u>ed</u>
load<u>ed</u>

English can have as many as four consonants in a word-final consonant cluster – 'texts' /teksts/ although colloquial speech may prefer to drop off (or *elide*) one of the elements for speed of delivery (e.g. 'waltzed' / wɔːltst / → / wɔːlst /). To build up your awareness of how these consonant clusters are made up, fill in the consonant worksheet in Exercise 7.

Exercise 7: Consonant Pattern

A. *How many consonant sounds do you make before the first vowel sound in the following words?*

e.g. <u>spl</u>ashed: <u>ccc</u> –

1.	scheme	11.	photo ....
2.	whose	12.	stew ....
3.	squirrel	13.	chaos ....
4.	gnome	14.	sphere ....
5.	science	15.	they ....
6.	choir	16.	throat ....
7.	shrewd	17.	huge ....
8.	swords	18.	squeeze ....
9.	pneumonia	19.	knew ....
10.	shock	20.	jaw ....

B. *How many consonant sounds do you make after the first vowel sound in the following words?*

e.g. spl<u>ashed</u>: – <u>cc</u>

1.	egged	11.	frill ....
2.	bathed	12.	depths ....
3.	lengths	13.	signed ....
4.	pushed	14.	rough ....
5.	sixth	15.	isles ....
6.	crumbs	16.	yachts ....
7.	mixed	17.	soothes ....
8.	halves	18.	yolks ....
9.	sphinx	19.	texts ....
10.	tongues	20.	twelfth ....

The vowel acts as the centre, or nucleus of the syllable, and there may be up to three consonants at the beginning of a word (in the word-initial cluster) and up to four consonants at the end (in the word-final cluster).

A formula to describe the syllable structure of English as presented by Abercrombie (1971) is:

$$C \qquad V \qquad C$$
$$0\text{–}3 \qquad\qquad 0\text{–}4$$

Now that the consonants of R.P. have been examined, the next section will look at the central, nuclear phonemes: the Vowels.

The Vowel System of R.P.

Vowels are produced with comparatively little restriction on the airstream in its passage through the vocal tract, although they are nearly always voiced. The differences in vowel quality are produced by changes in the shape of the oral cavity as the tongue takes up different contours in the mouth. The changes in tongue position produce different resonating cavities within which the airstream vibrates. The usual way to identify the tongue position is by describing the highest point of the tongue in the mouth (see Figure 8).

Vowels are classified into monophthongs or diphthongs. A monophthong is a pure vowel with no change in the vowel quality during production (/ ɑː / in 'laugh' / e / in 'red'). A diphthong can be described as a vowel glide of changing quality because the tongue moves from one tongue position to another during production (/ eɪ / in 'train', / aʊ / in 'cow').

Remember that accents may vary a great deal in their vowel systems, so listeners tend to be more tolerant of differences in vowel qualities than in changes in the consonants.

Description

Vowels are classified along three parameters depending on the highest point of the tongue and the lip position:

Parameter 1:

Front ——————— Central ——————— Back

If the highest point of the tongue is at the front of the mouth and fairly close to the roof (although not close enough to produce friction) the resulting vowel is / iː / ('key'). If on the other hand it is still high in the mouth but the highest point is towards the back, the vowel / uː / is produced ('coo').

'key' iː ————————————— uː 'coo'

/ iː / is therefore known as a *close front* vowel and / uː / as a *close back* vowel. They are both close because the highest point of the tongue is close to the hard palate (see Figure 8). The *central* vowel / ɜː / in 'bird' is produced with the tongue relaxed in the mouth.

Parameter 2:

The tongue is comprised of an extremely flexible set of muscles and can move not only backwards and forwards but also up and down in the mouth.

The high or close vowels are produced with the highest point of the tongue near the roof of the mouth (/ iː / in 'key') and the low or open

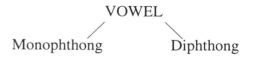

VOWEL

Monophthong   Diphthong

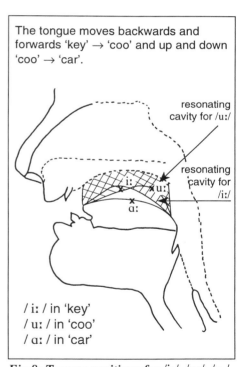

The tongue moves backwards and forwards 'key' → 'coo' and up and down 'coo' → 'car'.

resonating cavity for /uː/

resonating cavity for /iː/

/ iː / in 'key'
/ uː / in 'coo'
/ ɑː / in 'car'

Fig 8: Tongue positions for /iː/, /uː/, /ɑ/

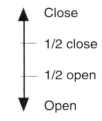

Close

1/2 close

1/2 open

Open

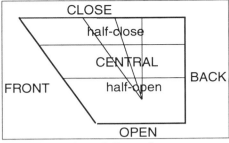

Fig. 9: Vowel quadrilateral

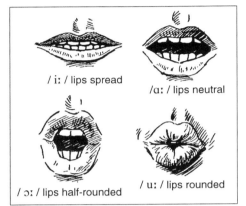

Fig. 10: Lip positions for vowels

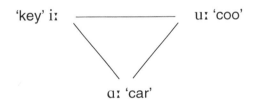

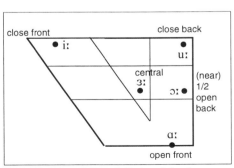

Fig. 11: Vowel Quadrilateral for long vowels.

vowels are produced with the highest point of the tongue low in the mouth (/ ɑː / in 'car').

Between these extremes is a large variety of other possible vowel qualities but a finite number of specific vowel phonemes selected to carry the meaningful contrasts in a particular language. Intermediate levels may be referred to as half close and half open. The vowel quadrilateral in Figure 9 represents the position of the highest point of the tongue for the vowels, described in terms of the two parameters outlined above.

Parameter 3

The third identifying characteristic of the vowels concerns the position of the lips (see Figure 10). They may be:

spread:	for	/ iː /	'sheep'
half spread:	for	/ ɪ /	'ship'
neutral:	for	/ e /	'hen', / ɑː / 'car'
half rounded:	for	/ ɔː /	'horse'
rounded:	for	/ uː /	'moon'

Based on the three parameters above

/ iː / may be classified as a close front vowel with lips spread
/ uː / is a close back vowel with lips rounded
/ ɑː / is an open back vowel with lips neutral

As in the case of the consonants, it is expected that learners will have a general understanding of how the vowels are classified rather than an ability to describe the tongue positions in detail. Vowel qualities are best learnt by imitation and monitoring and *not* from any theory or symbols on paper. It is therefore important to listen to the accompanying tape and to try to evaluate production in comparison to the spoken model.

The Monophthongs of R.P.

Monophthongs are pure vowels which may be long or short. Long vowels are indicated in the transcription by having two dots ː after the symbol (/ɑː/ in 'car', /iː/ in 'eel'). It is important that vowel quantity as well as quality is preserved in spoken English otherwise two phonemes may fall together (e.g. /ɪ/ in 'ship' and /iː/ in 'sheep').

English has five long vowels: /iː/ in 'sheep', /ɑː/ in 'car', /ɔː/ in 'horse', /uː/ in 'moon' and /ɜː/ in 'bird'.

These are represented on the quadrilateral in Figure 11.

Now do Exercise 8.

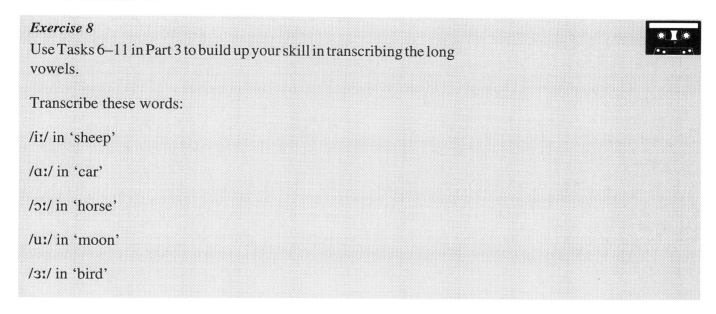

Exercise 8

Use Tasks 6–11 in Part 3 to build up your skill in transcribing the long vowels.

Transcribe these words:

/iː/ in 'sheep'

/ɑː/ in 'car'

/ɔː/ in 'horse'

/uː/ in 'moon'

/ɜː/ in 'bird'

The next stage is to add the short vowels in English. These are

/ ɪ / in 'ship'	/ ʌ / in 'cup'
/ e / in 'hen'	/ ɒ / in 'clock'
/ æ / in 'cat'	/ ʊ / in 'bull'

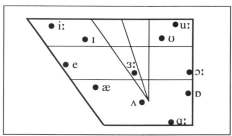

Fig. 12: Vowel Quadrilateral for short vowels

The tongue positions required for the production of these sounds lead to their plotting on the vowel quadrilateral (see Figure 12) which, as mentioned earlier, is simply a stylised representation of the position of the highest point of the tongue (see Figure 13) .

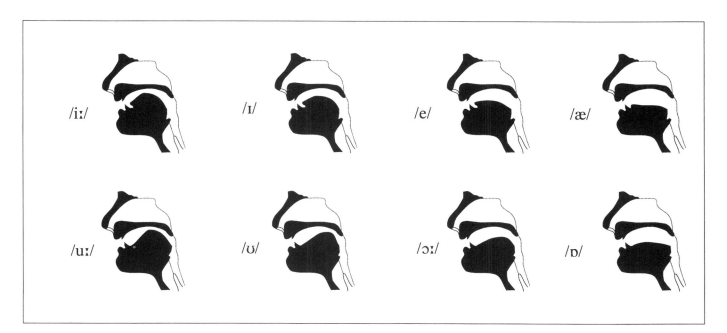

Fig. 13: Highest positions of the tongue for articulation of the vowels.

Working from high to low (close to open) down the left side, the front vowels on the quadrilateral will be as follows:

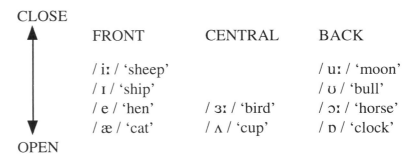

CLOSE

	FRONT	CENTRAL	BACK
	/ iː / 'sheep'		/ uː / 'moon'
	/ ɪ / 'ship'		/ ʊ / 'bull'
	/ e / 'hen'	/ ɜː / 'bird'	/ ɔː / 'horse'
	/ æ / 'cat'	/ ʌ / 'cup'	/ ɒ / 'clock'

OPEN

The tongue position for / ɪ / in 'ship' is slightly lower than / iː / in 'sheep' so the dot will be nearer the half-close position. Similarly / ɔː / in 'horse' is higher than / ɒ / in 'clock' so the dot to represent the long / ɔː / vowel will be plotted above the half-open position.

In order to get used to these symbols, transcribe the word lists and check vowel qualities against key words in Fig. 16 page 72. As you improve you should be able to dispense with the key word list. It is often easier to work from transcription into orthography so Exercise 9 below requires you to write the ordinary spelling of a series of words, whereas Exercise 10 requires you to transcribe the list.

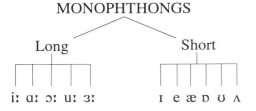

MONOPHTHONGS

Long — Short

iː ɑː ɔː uː ɜː   ɪ e æ ɒ ʊ ʌ

Now do Exercises 9 and 10.

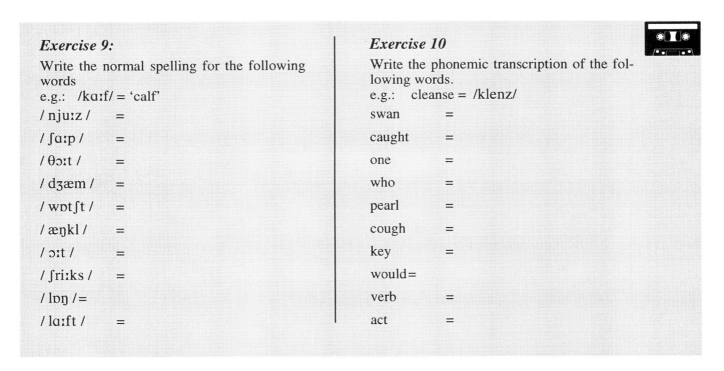

Exercise 9:
Write the normal spelling for the following words
e.g.: /kɑːf/ = 'calf'

/ njuːz /	=
/ ʃɑːp /	=
/ θɔːt /	=
/ dʒæm /	=
/ wɒtʃt /	=
/ æŋkl /	=
/ ɔːt /	=
/ ʃriːks /	=
/ lɒŋ /	=
/ lɑːft /	=

Exercise 10
Write the phonemic transcription of the following words.
e.g.: cleanse = /klenz/

swan	=
caught	=
one	=
who	=
pearl	=
cough	=
key	=
would	=
verb	=
act	=

For further practice, turn to Exercise 13 on page 22 and work through Tasks 13–21 in Part 3 (pages 96–100).

The Diphthongs of R.P.

Diphthongs of R.P. are classified into closing diphthongs and centring diphthongs.

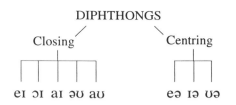

Closing dipthongs

During the production of this group, the tongue position moves up in the mouth towards a more close tongue position. These gliding vowels end in / ɪ / or / ʊ /, three in the first category – / eɪ /, / aɪ /, / ɔɪ / – and two in the second – / aʊ / and / əʊ /. They are:

/ eɪ / in 'train'	/ aʊ / in 'cow'
/ aɪ / in 'kite'	/ əʊ / in 'goat'
/ ɔɪ / in 'boy'	

Now do Exercise 11

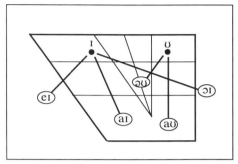

Fig. 14: Closing Diphthongs

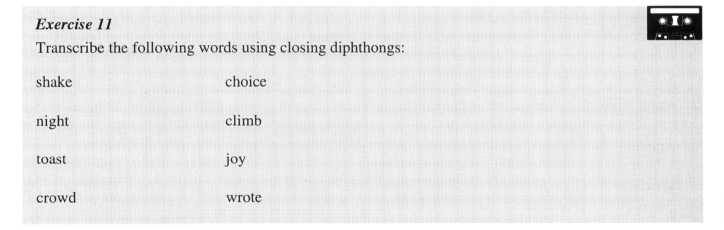

Exercise 11

Transcribe the following words using closing diphthongs:

shake	choice
night	climb
toast	joy
crowd	wrote

Centring diphthongs

The tongue position moves towards the central vowel /ə/ for the production of these three diphthongs. They are:

/ ɪə / in 'ear'
/ eə / in 'chair'
/ ʊə / in 'poor'

Notice that /ʊə/ is pronounced as /ɔː/ by many R.P. speakers. For example, 'sure' = /ʃɔː/ or /ʃʊə/.

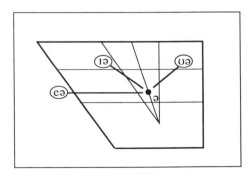

Fig. 15: Centring Diphthongs

Now do Exercise 12

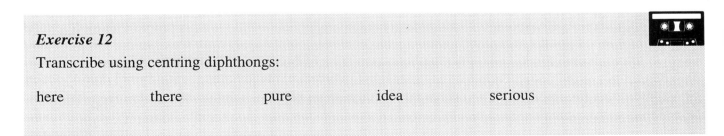

Exercise 12

Transcribe using centring diphthongs:

here	there	pure	idea	serious

Vowel sounds		Consonant sounds	
iː	b<u>ea</u>t	p	<u>p</u>at
ɪ	b<u>i</u>t	b	<u>b</u>at
e	b<u>e</u>t	t	<u>t</u>rot
æ	b<u>a</u>t	d	<u>d</u>ot
ɑː	f<u>a</u>ther	k	<u>k</u>i<u>ck</u>
ɒ	p<u>o</u>t	g	<u>g</u>ot
ɔː	p<u>or</u>t	m	<u>m</u>at
ʊ	b<u>u</u>ll	n	<u>n</u>ot
uː	z<u>oo</u>	ŋ	ri<u>ng</u>
ʌ	b<u>u</u>t	f	<u>f</u>at
ɜː	b<u>ur</u>n/	v	<u>v</u>at
eɪ	b<u>a</u>ke	θ	<u>th</u>ought
əʊ	b<u>oa</u>t	ð	<u>th</u>at
aɪ	b<u>i</u>te	s	<u>s</u>at
aʊ	b<u>ou</u>nd	z	<u>z</u>ero
ɔɪ	b<u>oy</u>	ʃ	<u>sh</u>ip
ɪə	b<u>eer</u>	ʒ	trea<u>s</u>ure
eə	b<u>ear</u>	tʃ	<u>ch</u>ew
ʊə	p<u>oor</u>	dʒ	<u>j</u>aw
		h	<u>h</u>at
		r	<u>r</u>at
		l	<u>l</u>ot
		w	<u>w</u>ish
		j	<u>y</u>es

Fig. 16: The phonemes of R.P.

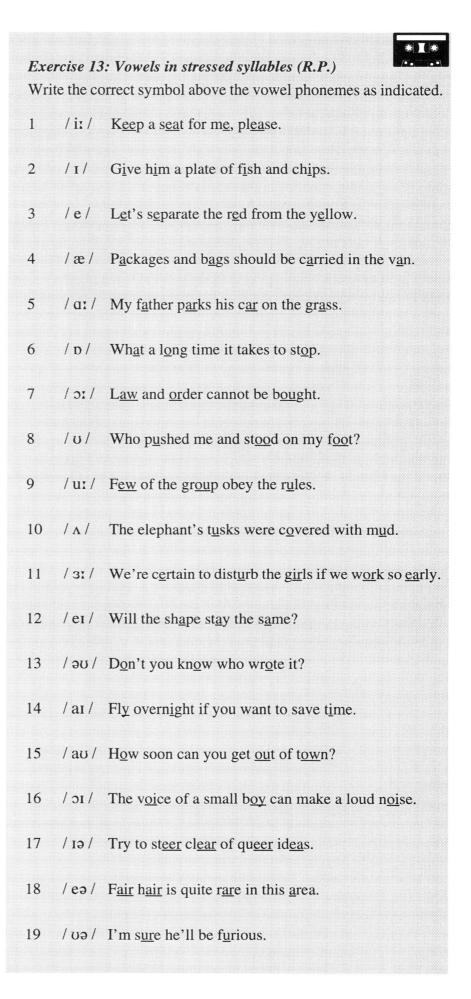

Exercise 13: Vowels in stressed syllables (R.P.)

Write the correct symbol above the vowel phonemes as indicated.

1 / iː / K<u>ee</u>p a s<u>ea</u>t for m<u>e</u>, pl<u>ea</u>se.

2 / ɪ / G<u>i</u>ve h<u>i</u>m a plate of f<u>i</u>sh and ch<u>i</u>ps.

3 / e / L<u>e</u>t's s<u>e</u>parate the r<u>e</u>d from the y<u>e</u>llow.

4 / æ / P<u>a</u>ckages and b<u>a</u>gs should be c<u>a</u>rried in the v<u>a</u>n.

5 / ɑː / My f<u>a</u>ther p<u>a</u>rks his c<u>a</u>r on the gr<u>a</u>ss.

6 / ɒ / Wh<u>a</u>t a l<u>o</u>ng time it takes to st<u>o</u>p.

7 / ɔː / L<u>aw</u> and <u>or</u>der cannot be b<u>ou</u>ght.

8 / ʊ / Who p<u>u</u>shed me and st<u>oo</u>d on my f<u>oo</u>t?

9 / uː / F<u>ew</u> of the gr<u>ou</u>p obey the r<u>u</u>les.

10 / ʌ / The elephant's t<u>u</u>sks were c<u>o</u>vered with m<u>u</u>d.

11 / ɜː / We're c<u>e</u>rtain to dist<u>u</u>rb the g<u>ir</u>ls if we w<u>or</u>k so <u>ear</u>ly.

12 / eɪ / Will the sh<u>a</u>pe st<u>ay</u> the s<u>a</u>me?

13 / əʊ / D<u>o</u>n't you kn<u>ow</u> who wr<u>o</u>te it?

14 / aɪ / Fl<u>y</u> overn<u>i</u>ght if you want to save t<u>i</u>me.

15 / aʊ / H<u>ow</u> soon can you get <u>ou</u>t of t<u>ow</u>n?

16 / ɔɪ / The v<u>oi</u>ce of a small b<u>oy</u> can make a loud n<u>oi</u>se.

17 / ɪə / Try to st<u>eer</u> cl<u>ear</u> of qu<u>eer</u> id<u>ea</u>s.

18 / eə / F<u>air</u> h<u>air</u> is quite r<u>are</u> in this <u>a</u>rea.

19 / ʊə / I'm s<u>ure</u> he'll be f<u>u</u>rious.

Connected Speech

Up to this point we have been looking at the individual meaningful sounds of the language, the *phonemes*, and how they combine within a single syllable. Now we will examine how syllables group together to make up the word and, more importantly, how they build up to form the typical rhythm of spoken English in the utterance. Speaker's meaning will then be considered with reference to main focus and we will look at the options at the disposal of the speaker which help to highlight the most important items in the message and background those of less significance.

Finally, there is a brief introduction to the area of intonation to explore how differences at this level provide an extra layer of meaning at the disposal of the speaker.

Word Stress

Spoken language is not made up of isolated words but of connected speech, and it is more important to examine the way in which words function in context than to look exhaustively at how they are constructed as discrete items. As soon as two or more syllables occur together, the concept of stress has to be taken into account. Some syllables are produced with extra effort (stressed syllables) whereas others are produced quickly and less distinctly (weak syllables).

Recognition of the stressed syllables of the language is important for comprehension and correct production is required for successful communication. From the listener's point of view, the stressed syllables are heard more loudly and the weakened syllables disappear into the background and are given little attention.

Research suggests that native speakers store words according to their stress-pattern, and that failure in word stress placement is more likely to lead to misunderstanding than an error at the level of the phoneme (Brown 1971).

The vowel in the stressed syllable usually has its full phonemic value, whereas if it occurs in an unstressed syllable, it will become centralised and weakened.

Stressed	*Stressed + Weak*
'land /'lænd/	'Scotland /'skɒtlənd/
'berry /'berɪ/	'strawberry /'strɔːbərɪ/.

The characteristic vowel of the weakened syllable is called *schwa* and the symbol used for it is / ə /. This schwa vowel is the most common phoneme in the phonology of English because it occurs so frequently.

/ɪn ðə fənɒlədʒɪ əv ðə læŋgwɪdʒ/

SYLLABLE

stressed (loud)= reinforced chest pulse   weak (quiet)= ordinary chest pulse

23

Learners who tend to give equal stress to each syllable in a word like 'lecturer' (lec-tu-rer) will have great difficulty in reducing the weak syllables sufficiently to pronounce /ˈlektʃərə/. This will have implications for their listening skills since lack of exposure to native-speaker English may not prepare the learner to guess at the meaning of the ubiquitous reductions in vowel quality. Many students who arrive in Britain for the first time complain that speakers "swallow half their words". The lack of vowel clarity due to the frequency of the /ə/ confuses them.

Stress in the Syllables

Before embarking on a brief examination of word stress, it is important to define the syllable. Listeners can often guess at the number of syllables in a word (A-me-ri-ca = 4; Ca-na-da = 3; pro-nun-ci-a-tion = 5) as they are recognising a certain number of beats or pulses. The airstream exits from the lungs not in a steady flow but in a series of short pulses or syllables. Some of these chest pulses are produced with extra effort (reinforced chest pulses) and result in stressed syllables, whereas others are produced with little effort (ordinary chest pulses) and result in weak syllables.

The word 'photographer', for example, has four syllables (pho-to-gra-pher), one stressed syllable (pho'tographer) and three weak syllables (phŏ 'to gră phĕr).

All words of one syllable are stressed in isolation. Word stress operates in words of more than one syllable, that is to say in polysyllabic words.

Two-syllable words have two possible patterns:

   — •   • —

 (stressed and weak)   (weak and stressed)

Up to 90% of disyllabic (two-syllable) *nouns* will have their stress on the first syllable, the other syllable becoming weakened to /ə/ or /ɪ/. Disyllabic *verbs* on the other hand, are more likely to take the stress on the second syllable and weaken the first syllable if they start with a prefix.

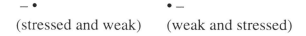

— •	• —
'Scotland	pre'fer
'father	con'fess
'carpet	de'cide
'cupboard	re'fuse

Four Syllables:
ONE STRESSED SYLLABLE

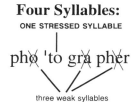

phŏ 'to gră phĕr

three weak syllables

Now do Exercise 14.

Exercise 14: Word stress patterns (two syllables)

Listen to the following words on tape and mark the stress with the sign immediately before the stressed syllable (e.g. 'second, be'fore). Write the weakened vowel /ə/ or /ɪ/ above the unstressed syllable in the word (e.g. 'father, sur'prise).

— •	• —		— •	• —
father	surprise		after	appear
carpet	today		August	escape
likely	perhaps		peaceful	asleep
helpful	ahead		under	complain
Monday	discuss		reading	prefer

Now add the following words to the correct column: compare, easy, happy, valley, succeed, autumn, teacher, release:

— •　　　　• —

There is a special group of two syllable words where the function of the word is signalled by the position of the stress.

—• *noun*	•— *verb*
'subject /'sʌbdʒɪkt/	sub'ect /səb'dʒekt/
'object	ob'ject
'convict	con'vict
'transport	trans'port
'export	ex'port

Three-syllable words (Trisyllabic) have three possible patterns:

— •	• — •	• • —
'lecturer	ex'ample	under'stand
'mystery	dis'cussion	engi'neer

Notice that three syllable words of the pattern ••— usually have a secondary stress (full value vowel) on the first syllable: /ˌʌndəˈstænd/

Now do Exercises 15–19.

Exercise 15: Word Stress

1. Look at the following list of polysyllabic words and see whether you can mark the stress correctly.
2. Listen to the list on tape and check your analysis.
3. Look at the check-list provided on pages 43 and 44 and correct your version.

2-syllables

decide	module		
purpose	attach		
idea	details		
described	technique		
practice	correct		

3-syllables

examples	rationale
lecturer	clarify
discussion	implement
indicate	relevant
overseas	connecting

4-syllables

circumstances	integrated
competition	original
estimated	psychology
particular	activities
appropriate	comprehension

5-syllables

accommodation	opportunity
technicality	vocabulary
characteristic	communicative
international	supplementary

Short Phrases

communicative activities	grammatical weaknesses
international language	complete micro-teaching reports
evaluation and assessment	concepts of collocation
appropriacy of techniques	optional objectives
particular teaching situation	

For a useful list of word stress rules see Rogerson and Gilbert (1990, p. 23).

Exercise 16

Find other examples of (a) animals and (b) countries to fit the following patterns:

_ •	• _	_ ••	• _ •	•• _
'monkey	ba'boon	'crocodile	h'yena	chimpan'zee
'England	Ja'pan	'Germany	Ja'maica	Pakis'tan

Exercise 17

Using a dictionary, find cognate forms of the following and indicate the word stress:

noun	*adjective*	*verb*
'family	fa'miliar	to familia'rise
so'ciety	. . . .	. . . .
. . . .	o'riginal	. . . .
. . . .	. . . .	to com'pete
edu'cation	. . . .	. . . .

Exercise 18

Collect all of the polysyllabic words (words of more than one syllable) in the following passage and mark their word stress.

The North Wind and the Sun

The North Wind and the Sun were disputing which was the stronger, when a traveller came along wrapped in a warm cloak. They agreed that the one who first succeeded in making the traveller take his cloak off should be considered stronger than the other. Then the North Wind blew as hard as he could, but the more he blew the more closely did the traveller fold his cloak around him; and at last the North Wind gave up the attempt. Then the Sun shone out warmly, and immediately the traveller took off his cloak. And so the North Wind was obliged to confess that the Sun was the stronger of the two.

Exercise 19

Here is the transcription of the last sentence:

/ənd səʊ ðə nɔːθ wɪnd wəz əblaɪdʒd tə kənfes ðət ðə sʌn wəz ðə strɒngər əv ðə tuː/

Rhythm

Abercrombie (1961) observed that all speech is essentially rhythmical. Any rhythm involves the regular recurrence of a beat and in the spoken medium the rhythm is created by the regularity of either the ordinary syllables or the stressed syllables. Languages are termed syllable-timed if the ordinary syllable recurs regularly and most syllables receive equal force. Examples of syllable-timed languages are Italian, French, Swahili, Japanese. If there is a tendency for the stressed syllables to follow each other at roughly equal intervals of time, the language is termed stressed-timed. English, German, Russian and Arabic belong to this second category of languages.

There has been some continuing discussion since Bolinger's comments in 1965 as to whether the concept of strict stress-timing is tenable. Most authorities agree with Taylor (1981), however, that English 'has an overwhelming tendency towards regular alternation of stressed and unstressed syllables and that this produces the impression of a regular rhythmic beat which the listener tends to perceive as isochronous.' While accepting that the term 'stress-timed' is a useful concept, Taylor goes on to caution: 'provided we do not take it too seriously and think of it rather as non-syllable-timed rhythm'. The beats follow each other with some regularity in English although increasing numbers of syllables between the beats will undoubtedly cause a slightly longer interval to elapse before the next down-beat.

It is certainly true of English that there is a marked difference in the vowel quality between the stressed and the weakened syllables in spoken English. Learners from a syllable-timed background will have difficulties not only at word-level but also in longer stretches of text. English listeners tend to rely on the clear placement of the stress both in the polysyllabic word and, even more importantly, in the stream of speech where the stressed syllables are used to identify the information-bearing items in the utterance. The function of stress in the utterance can therefore be said to be to cue the words necessary to ensure successful transfer of the speaker's meaning.

In a sentence like 'Look at the mark on the door', the words 'look' 'mark' and 'door' are all important for correct understanding:

LOOK MARK DOOR

As long as the listener has heard these, he can guess at the meaning of the rest of the utterance. These important content words will usually belong to the categories of nouns, verbs, adjectives and adverbs.

The other group, the structural words (the prepositions, conjunction, articles) will fall into the background and become weakened by comparison. Once again the /ə/ vowel is involved, this time to realise weak forms of structural words.

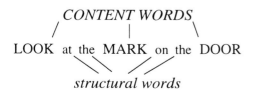

In Part 1 we are going to concentrate on recognition of the stressed syllables and in Part 2 we will move on to look at what happens in the unstressed syllables in English.

The usual convention to show word-stress is to use a small diacritic (dia'critic) before the stressed syllable, in line with dictionary usage. The rhythm, however, will be marked with slashes similar to the beat in music:

> / Look at the   / mark on the   / door
> *unit of rhythm*   *unit of rhythm*   *unit of rhythm*
> (foot)   (foot)   (foot)

Each downbeat starts a new bar of music or rhythm group called 'the foot'. The foot starts with a stressed syllable and contains all the following unstressed syllables up to the next stress. Notice that the rhythmic bar must co-occur with the word-stress:

> The /sun be/gan to /shine as he a/rrived.

Now do Exercises 20–21.

Exercise 20

Mark the rhythm in the exercise. Remember that the beat (the slash) will usually be placed before the stressed syllable of a content word.

e.g. /This is the /third of Ju/ly
E/xams are /difficult for /everyone

1. He wants to go to college.

2. I eat an apple every day.

3. When are they coming to meet you?

4. The lady was young and attractive.

5. Does Grandfather want us to go to the concert?

6. Put a stamp on the envelope.

7. We'll come tomorrow morning if you like.

8. I thought it was an excellent decision.

9. Where did you put the packet of biscuits?

10. The sun began to shine as he arrived.

11. Give me a piece of cake, please.

12. I don't believe a word he says.

13. Don't believe him, whatever he says.

14. The exercise is easy.

15. Exams are difficult for everyone.

Exercise 21

Listen again to the passage the 'North Wind and the Sun'. This time mark the rhythm by placing the slashes before the stressed syllables. Make sure that you observe the word-stress conventions as well.

Example: The /North /Wind and the /Sun were dis/puting /which was the /stronger, when a /traveller came a/long /wrapped in a /warm /cloak. They a/greed . . .

Remember that most lexical items (nouns, verbs, adjectives) will be stressed and that the structural items are unlikely to carry a beat (in normal circumstances).

The North Wind and the Sun

The North Wind and the Sun were disputing which was the stronger, when a traveller came along wrapped in a warm cloak. They agreed that the one who first succeeded in making the traveller take his cloak off should be considered stronger than the other. Then the North Wind blew as hard as he could, but the more he blew the more closely did the traveller fold his cloak around him; and at last the North Wind gave up the attempt. Then the Sun shone out warmly, and immediately the traveller took off his cloak. And so the North Wind was obliged to confess that the Sun was the stronger of the two.

Poems build up our expectation of where the beat will occur. The stress is particularly noticeable and structured and therefore poems (or nursery rhymes) provide excellent teaching materials for learners.

Young learner

— ∪ — ∪ — ∪ —
/Jack and /Jill went /up the /hill

Advanced learner

∪ — ∪ — ∪ — ∪ — ∪ —
The / curfew / tolls the / knell of / parting / day

As you will see in the above example, each foot in poetry often contains the same number of syllables and this establishes a rhythmic formality.

Exercise 22

Listen to the poem *The House that Jack Built* and look at the marking of the rhythm.

The House that Jack Built
/This is the /house that /Jack /built.
/This is the /malt
That /lay in the /house that /Jack /built.
/This is the /rat,
That /ate the /malt
That /lay in the /house that /Jack /built.
/This is the /cat,
That /killed the /rat,
That /ate the /malt
That /lay in the /house that Jack /built.

Now listen to the recording of Edward Lear's rhyme and mark the beats:

There was a young lady of Riga

Who went for a ride on a tiger.

They finished their ride

With the lady inside

And a smile on the face of the tiger.

Listening to a spoken text has a parallel in skimming a written text where one is looking for gist. We listen for the important words to be given extra stress and retrieve the meaning of the low-information words from context, filling in the gaps from our background experience in the language and culture. The aim is to develop global comprehension in listening and it is unnecessary for us to hear every word clearly.

Main Focus

Whilst it is true to say that all content words are likely to be stressed in English, it is also the case that some stresses are more important than others. This observation leads into another crucial area for successful transfer of the message. The speaker cues the listener into the item in the utterance he considers most vital for correct interpretation of his meaning by placing his *main focus* on that item. Main focus involves increased stress, longer vowel quality on the syllable but, most important of all, it carries the major pitch change in the unit of information. It is this location of the pitch movement which has most significance. For example:

> I /always /fly to /France in the /Spring
> (neutral = expected placement towards end of the unit)

However, depending on the stimulus, the speaker might select one of the other items as his most appropriate response in that context:

> (Stimulus) Are you going to France in the Spring?
>
> (Response) Yes. I always fly to France in the Spring.
>
> (Stimulus) Are you going by car this year?
>
> (Response) No. I always fly to France in the Spring.
>
> (Stimulus) Is it Switzerland this year?
>
> (Response) No. I always fly to France in the Spring.

(Note that if one word were to be sufficient response, it would be the item carrying the main focus.)

This is clearly a vital feature for learners to cue into, both as listeners and as speakers. English uses this device to highlight important information where other languages might use, for example, a change in word order.

If we think about the relative importance which a speaker accords to his information, we can conclude that:

- All content words are of central importance and therefore *stressed*.

- Structural items are not essential and are therefore *backgrounded* by being weakened

- The most crucial item for successful transfer of information is given extra *prominence* by carrying the major pitch movement on the stressed syllable. Other features are also present to reinforce the location such as extra loudness and a lengthened vowel, but the main clue is the placement of the pitch change. Frequently an extralinguistic gesture such as raised eyebrows or a nod of the head is also present to provide an additional visual signal.

Summary

FOCUS: Most Important item	*SPRING*
HIGHLIGHT: Content words	. . . always . . . fly . . . France . . .
BACKGROUND: Structural items	X̶ always fly t̶o̶ France i̶n̶ t̶h̶e̶ *SPRING.*

The most likely position for main focus is towards the end of the unit since it is often carries the new information in the context (that is, the information not already known, or "given", to the listener). Consequently, the placement of main focus on the last lexical item is regarded as neutral, or expected. Note that it must be on the last lexical item and not on a structural word. Many learners make the mistake of placing it on the last word in a sentence as in,

If I <u>see</u> him // I'll ask <u>him</u>

where the emphasis on 'him' would have special implications for English speakers who would immediately assume that 'him' was being contrasted to 'her' or 'us'.

Now do Exercise 23

Exercise 23

Listen to the following examples and underline the syllable containing the main focus on the last lexical item:

e.g.   All men are born <u>e</u>qual.

1.   He works at the British Council.

2.   Her husband is a doctor.

3.   Please would you sign it.

4.   Which city do you prefer?

5.   They're attending a lecture.

6.   You must finish the assignment by Friday.

When the main focus is placed on one of the other content words, the listener has to pick up on the implication because the speaker has changed it for a reason. The alternative positions are known as **marked placement** and change the implication of the message. It is necessary to understand the context in order to predict where marked placement will occur. There is no single correct position but placement may be negotiated during a conversation. Decisions about location will relate to *new* and *given* as mentioned above or they may relate to contrast or confirmation. In other words, the speaker will make on-going decisions about which item will carry the main focus during an interaction and will negotiate new information, contrast or confirmation depending on the context.

For example:

A	I'm looking for a <u>book</u>.
B	What <u>kind</u> of book?
A	One with some <u>recipes</u>.
B	Do you like It<u>al</u>ian recipes?
A	<u>No</u> thanks. I prefer <u>French.</u>

In this way, decisions about location are on-going and depend on the appropriateness to context. The listener should be constantly on the alert and ready to pick up the significance of changes in focus.

In each of the cases, illustrated in Figure 17, the pitch movement remains the same (a falling pitch for a statement of fact) but the location of the movement changes and signals important alterations in meaning.

Now do Exercises 24–27.

Fig. 17: The location of pitch movement alters meaning.

marked   neutral

All men are born equal

— but some work hard to succeed

— confirmation they *are!*

— but what about women?

— not only the favoured few gathered here today

Exercise 24

Locate the main focus in the following examples (e.g. Would <u>you</u> like another drink?). Only underline the syllable which carries the main focus in the word being identified. This takes account of the rules of word stress.

1. I'll ask Mary to come.

2. Does he always arrive before the meal?

3. Fry the bananas in butter.

4. Think of a word beginning with 'B'.

5. They've never watered their plants.

6. I'd like to invite her husband as well.

Exercise 25

Listen to the story of 'The Lion and the Hare'. It is already marked for rhythm. Underline the words which you think carry the main focus because they stand out as they are spoken more loudly and because they carry a pitch movement.

The Lion and The Hare

/Once a /lion /found a /hare. He was /just /going to /eat her when /a stag /ran /by.

'/That /stag will /make me a /bigger /dinner,' he /said.

/So he /let the /hare /go and ran /after the /stag/. But the /stag could /run /very, /very /fast and /soon it got /right a/way.

/When the /lion /saw that he /could not /catch the /stag, he /said, 'I will /go /back for the /hare.'

But /when he /came to the /place where the /hare had /been, he /found that she had /gone.

'I /should have /had her for my /dinner when I /first /saw her,' /said the /lion. 'I /wanted /too /much and /now I have /nothing.'

Thought Groups

Notice how the reader of the story 'The Lion and the Hare' pauses meaningfully. We call these groupings into meaningful units 'thought groups' or 'sense groups'.

Each group will contain an item of main focus and be characterised by carrying a pitch movement (or tone). Speakers break up the stream of speech into these coherent chunks and pause to allow their listeners to process meaning.

Thought groups play a central role in delineating information structures and will be examined in greater detail in Part 2. For present purposes, think of them as being bounded by pauses and mark them on paper with double slashes.

Exercise 26

Listen to the story of 'The Lion and the Hare' and notice rhythm and thought groups.

// Once a /lion /found a /hare. // He was /just /going to /eat her // when /a stag /ran /by. //

/'That /stag will /make me a /bigger /dinner,' // he /said. //

/So he /let the /hare /go // and /ran /after the /stag. // But the /stag could /run /very, /very /fast // and /soon it got /right a/way. //

/When the /lion /saw // that he /could not /catch /the stag, // he /said, // 'I will /go /back for the /hare.' //

But /when he /came to the /place where the /hare had /been, // he /found that she had /gone. //

'I /should have /had her for my /dinner when I /first /saw her,' // /said the /Lion.// 'I /wanted /too /much // and /now I have /nothing.' //

Exercise 27

Listen to the text starting 'I want to tell you'.

a) Start by marking the rhythm with single slashes:
   I /want to /tell you /how to /get from /Rome to /Paris...

b) Mark the thought groups with double lines:
   //I/want to /tell you /how to /get from /Rome// to /Paris//...

c) Finally underline the main focus in each group:
   //I /want to /tell you /how to /get from /<u>Rome</u>// to /<u>Paris</u>//...

As you mark the main focus, think about the speaker's reasons for placement (new or given? contrast?)

I want to tell you how to get from Rome to Paris. Either go by plane, which is quick but costs a lot; or take a train which is slower but also cheaper; or go in your own car – if you have a car; or travel by bus, if you haven't a car, or don't want to drive yourself. I myself like to see the country when I travel, so I don't go by air unless I'm in a hurry. I haven't a car, so I have to choose the train or the bus. Most people, of course, go by train, because the idea of going from one country to another by bus is still rather strange. But I myself usually go by bus when I don't fly. I have plenty of time on these occasions, and enjoy seeing the village streets and the life that goes on along the less important country roads.

So far, we have been looking at how the speaker signals relative degrees of importance to his listener. Generally speaking, it is true to say that the more important an item is for successful transfer of the message, the more it will be stressed and placed in a position of prominence. This is in line with the way in which the child acquires phonological patterning because the first one-word utterances of the child will be the main item for focus:

JUICE

Later, other content words will appear:

want drink JUICE

and only at a later date, the adult version will develop with the structural items:

I **want** a **drink** of **JUICE** (please)

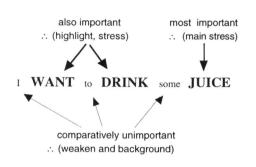

juice	*major focus*	= main stress and pitch movement
... want... drink...	*highlight*	= all content words
I.. to... some...	*background*	= structural items

Intonation

Intonation is frequently compared to music because it involves the rises and falls of the pitch of the voice, the 'melody'. Pitch is regulated by the frequency of vibration of the vocal cords and pitch pattens are used phonemically to differentiate between grammatical functions and also to add information about a speaker's attitude to his message. Meaning therefore involves not only the lexis and structures but also the intonation pattern selected by the speaker as the most appropriate for conveying his intention. In fact, the real meaning of a word or sentence could be totally reversed if, for example, 'wonderful' ☹ ↘ was said sarcastically with a low falling pitch instead of the cheerful 'exclamation mark' expected by the lexis and realised as a rising-falling pitch ↘↗ 'wonderful!' ☺

In the last few pages, we have looked at speaker's choices in terms of the following:

(a) How he packages his message by means of thought groups // I'd like to come// if I'm allowed'

(b) How he selects the most important item for main focus //I'd like to <u>come</u>// if I'm all<u>owed</u> //.

Now we are going to examine:

(c) How he selects an appropriate pitch movement to accompany the utterance.

The pitch movement in intonation can be regarded as having both grammatical and attitudinal functions. In Part 1 we will confine the discussion to the grammatical functions. Attitudinal function will be examined in Part 2 once a basis in the area has been established.

Basic Pitch Movements

The first basic division is between a falling ↘ and a rising ↗ pitch pattern. The distinction can be readily demonstrated by a short dialogue.

O.<u>K</u>.? ↗
O.<u>K</u>. ↘
<u>Com</u>ing? ↗
<u>Com</u>ing ↘
<u>Right</u>. <u>You</u> go first

It is clear from the above that the high rise is used for questions and the fall is used for statements of fact. Some writers (e.g. Rogerson and Gilbert) refer to open and closed which is a helpful distinction. 'Closed' simply means that the topic is not open for negotiation. It is certain or complete. 'Open' means that some sort of response is required from the listener or that the statement is incomplete. In other words it is unfinished.

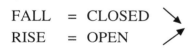

FALL = CLOSED ↘
RISE = OPEN ↗

Falling Pitch
Statements <u>and</u> Wh - questions

High rising pitch
Yes/No questions

Wh- questions (Who? Where? Why? How many?) normally use a falling pitch:

When did you ar<u>rive</u>?

Now do Exercise 28.

Exercise 28

Listen to the following sentences, and notice how the arrow is placed above the item of main focus. Then listen to the dialogues and mark the main focus and pitch arrows.

e.g.   She's the eldest in the <u>fam</u>ily.

        Do you take <u>sug</u>ar in your tea?

        When will you ar<u>rive</u>?

    A.   Hell<u>o</u>. Are you <u>new</u> here?

    B.   <u>Yes</u>. I just arrived on <u>Fri</u>day. Can you show me the way to the <u>li</u>brary, please?

DIALOGUE A

Loue: What do you want to eat, Aini? Would you like some rice?

Aini: Yes, please. And I'd like some vegetables.

Loue: Do you want some potatoes?

Aini: Yes please. What do you have to drink?

Loue: I've got some juice.

DIALOGUE B

Frans: I'm very happy today.

George: Why?

Frans: Because it's Sports Day.

George: Oh yes. Do you like sports?

Frans: Yes, I do. I'm good at sports. Do you like sports?

George: Not much. I'm not very good at them.

39

Tag Questions

These follow the same general pattern:

falling = confirming
rising = genuine question.

You're from Singapore, aren't you?=simply confirming what is already suspected. Speaker is fairly sure.

You're from Singapore, aren't you?=genuine question requiring a response. Speaker is unsure.

Now do Exercise 29.

Exercise 29

Listen to the following sentences and try to decide whether the speaker is *sure* or *unsure*:

e.g.   Sheridan wrote 'The Rivals', didn't he? *(sure)*

Obviously it is important for participants in a conversation to be able to read signals of this type accurately. For this reason intonation patterns can be regarded as turn-taking devices in discourse.

1. You've practised some transcription, haven't you?

2. Edinburgh's the capital of Scotland, isn't it?

3. They think intonation is a difficult area, don't they?

4. This is a real question, isn't it?

5. We've covered a lot of phonology here, haven't we?

6. You understand it a bit better now, don't you?

Low Rising and Level Pitch

There are a number of contexts where the low rise is the appropriate pattern, particularly if:

(a)   information is incomplete and there is more to come.

// Her/father's a/ doctor// and her / mother's a / teacher//

I'd / like some / apples // a / bunch of ba/nanas // and a melon

or

(b)   this is a polite request

//would you / open the / <u>win</u>dow / please//

//come / in and / sit / <u>down</u> //

To use a falling pitch in the examples in (b) above could sound rude whereas the low-rising movement for the request sounds encouraging and polite. In this way intonation patterns can be regarded as relating to the roles played by participants in any conversation. A dominant, authoritative figure would be likely to use high falling pitch movements to instruct the other interlocutor who might assume an inferior, anxious role using low rises (and fall-rises which suggest doubt and reservation).

We have now looked at some of the grammatical functions of intonation by examining how three different pitch curves are used in English. They are:

1. Fall   ↘   = statement/wh- questions

2. High Rise   ↗   = Yes/No questions

3. Low Rise   ↗   = Incomplete

In Part 2 we move on to re-examine these and to add more patterns determined by speaker's attitude

For present purposes of analysis, it has been necessary to adopt a seemingly artificial approach by extracting specific phonological features from the stream of speech and examining them separately. However, it cannot be over-emphasised that real speech takes place in context with all the potential for confusion for the non-native speaker that this implies.

There is no simple graded approach to phonology as there is in the case of lexis and grammar where a few words and structures may be introduced gradually and a larger repertoire carefully built up over an extended period. As soon as a speaker opens his mouth, all the phonological features are immediately present. Vowels, clusters, pitch height, weak forms, pitch movements, consonants, content words – all tumble out in a tightly-knit whole. All of the systems occur concurrently and it is not surprising that listeners may have difficulty in sorting through the stream and confused teachers ask: 'Where do we begin?'

The answer, of course, is to view the sound system as a central and indivisible part of language acquisition. As learners are introduced to the simple past tense, the various phonological realisations of the {-ed} ending are also encountered. As functions and notions are discussed, accompanying intonation patterns form part of the clue to meaning. It would be unwise to introduce new items of vocabulary without a concern for the word-stress placement which allows learners to 'pigeon-hole' the item under the correct pattern.

Real speech is connected speech occurring in a context. A true understanding of a speaker's meaning can only be gained through an awareness of how a particular utterance functions as part of the interaction as a whole, how it links to what has gone before and how it leads on to the topic to follow. Concepts of *new* and *given*, of appropriateness and of attitude are all essential ingredients in the discourse and many of these clues are carried by the phonological data. The speaker operates a surprisingly sophisticated system and has a vast potential reservoir for choice at his disposal. The listener needs to be alert to these nuances and finer points of the message and to interpret any deviations from the expected. It is our remit as describers of the language to pinpoint those variables and to explain them in terms of underlying meaning. An intuitive response may be perfectly valid but is insufficient in itself to satisfy the more curious learner. It is a central part of our equipment as teachers to be able to analyse, to explain and to relate observations to the theoretical framework within which the discourse operates. We have to understand the rules of the game and be skilful enough to hand them on to our learners.

Summary

Summary of Analysis of Connected Speech to date

*1. All the content words will be stressed (rhythm units = **feet**, marked by single slashes).*
In the /second /part of this /book we will e/xamine into/nation /patterns in /greater /detail.

*2. The utterance is divided into units of meaning (**thought groups**, marked by double slashes)*
//In the /second /part of this /book // we will e/xamine into/nation /patterns // in /greater /detail.//

*3. Each thought group will contain at least one focal point, essential for meaning (**main focus**, underlined).*
//In the /second /part of this /book // we will e/xamine into/nation /patterns // in /greater /detail.//

4. Select an appropriate pitch movement to accompany the main focus.

//In the /second /part of this /book // we will e/xamine into/nation /patterns // in /greater /detail.//
more to come   more to come   finish

Answers to Exercises in Part 1

Exercise 1

/b/   voiced labial stop
/k/   voiceless velar stop
/m/   voices labial nasal
/ŋ/   voiced velar nasal

Exercise 2

/n/, /p/, /g/, /d/

Exercise 3

CVC, CV, CVC, VC, CVC, CV

Exercise 4

CCVC, CCVC, CCCVC, CCCV, CCVC, CCVC, CCV

Exercise 5

/ɪz/, /z/, /s/, /z/, /s/, /ɪz/

Exercise 6

/d/, /t/, /ɪd/, /ɪd/, /t/, /d/

Exercise 7

A: 1:2, 2:1, 3:3, 4:1, 5:1, 6:2, 7:2, 8:1, 9:2, 10:1, 11:1, 12:3, 13:1, 14:2, 15:1, 16:2, 17:2, 18:3, 19:2, 20:1

B: 1:2, 2:2, 3:3/4, 4:2, 5:3, 6:2, 7:3, 8:2, 9:3, 10:2, 11:1, 12:3, 13:2, 14:1, 15:2, 16:2, 17:2, 18:2, 19:4, 20:3

Exercise 8

/ʃiːp/, /kɑː/, /hɔːs/, /muːn/, bɜːd/

Exercise 9

news, sharp, thought, jam, watched, ankle, ought, shrieks, long, laughed

Exercise 10

/swɒn/, /kɔːt/, /wʌn/, /huː/, /pɜːl/, /kɒf/, /kiː/, /wʊd/, /vɜːb/, /ækt/

Exercise 11

/ʃeɪk/, /naɪt/, təʊst/, /kraʊd/, /tʃɔɪs/, /klaɪm/, /dʒɔɪ/, /rəʊt/

Exercise 12

/hɪə/, /pjʊə/, /sɪərɪəs/, /ðeə/, /aɪdɪə/

Exercise 14

—•   easy, happy, valley, autumn, teacher
•—   compare, succeed, release

Exercise 15

2-syllables: de'cide, 'purpose, i'dea, des'cribed, 'practice, 'module, a'ttach, 'details, tech'nique, co'rrect

3-syllables: e'xamples, 'lecturer, dis'cussion, 'indicate, over'seas, ratio'nale, 'clarify, imple'ment, 'relevant, co'nnecting

4-syllables: 'circumstances, compe'tition, 'estimated, par'ticular, a'ppropriate, 'integrated, o'riginal, psy'chology, ac'tivities, compre'hension

5-syllables: accommo'dation, techni'cality, characte'ristic, inter'national, oppor'tunity, vo'cabulary, co'mmunicative, supple'mentary

Short phrases: co'mmunicative ac'tivities, inter'national 'language, evalu'ation and a'ssessment, a'ppropriacy of tech'niques, par'ticular 'teaching situ'ation, gra'mmatical 'weaknesses, com'plete 'micro-'teaching re'ports, 'concepts of collo'cation, 'optional ob'jectives

Exercise 16
The students' answers will vary.

Exercise 17
so'ciety, 'social, to 'socialise
'origin, o'riginal, to o'riginate
compe'tition, com'petitive, to com'pete
edu'cation, edu'cational, to 'educate

Exercise 18
See answer to Exercise 21.

Exercise 20
1. He /wants to /go to /college
2. I /eat an /apple /every /day
3. /When are they /coming to /meet you
4. The /lady was /young and a/ttractive
5. Does /Grandfather /want us to /go to the /concert
6. /Put a /stamp on the /envelope
7. We'll /come to/morrow /morning if you /like
8. I /thought it was an /excellent de/cision
9. /Where did you /put the /packet of /biscuits
10. The /sun be/gan to /shine as he a/rrived
11. /Give me a /piece of /cake /please
12. I /don't be/lieve a /word he /says
13. /Don't be/lieve him what/ever he /says
14. The /exercise is /easy
15. E/xams are /difficult for /everyone

Exercise 21
The /North /Wind and the/Sun
The /North /Wind and the/ Sun were dis/puting /which was the /stronger, when a /traveller came a/long /wrapped in a /warm /cloak. They a/greed that the /one who /first suc/ceeded in /making the /traveller /take his /cloak /off should be con/sidered /stronger than the /other. /Then the /North /Wind /blew as /hard as he /could, but the /more he /blew the /more /closely did the /traveller /fold his /cloak a/round him; and at /last the /North /Wind gave /up the a/ttempt. /Then the /Sun /shone /out /warmly, and i/mmediately the /traveller took /off his /cloak. And /so the /North /Wind was o/bliged to con/fess that the /Sun was the /stronger of the /two.

Exercise 22

There /was a young /lady of /Riga
Who /went for a /ride on a /tiger.
They /finished their /ride
With the /lady in/side
And a /smile on the /face of the /tiger.

Exercise 23

1. He works at the British <u>Coun</u>cil.
2. Her husband is a <u>doc</u>tor.
3. Please would you <u>sign</u> it.
4. Which city do you pre<u>fer</u>?
5. They're attending a <u>lec</u>ture.
6. You must finish your assignment by <u>Fri</u>day.

Exercise 24

1. I'll ask <u>Ma</u>ry to come.
2. Does he <u>al</u>ways arrive before the meal?
3. Fry the bananas in <u>but</u>ter.
4. Think of a word beginning with '<u>B</u>'.
5. They've <u>nev</u>er watered their plants.
6. I'd like to invite her <u>hus</u>band as well.

Exercise 25

Once a lion found a <u>hare</u>.//He was just going to <u>eat</u> her when a <u>stag</u> ran by.//
'That stag will make me a bigger <u>din</u>ner,'//he <u>said</u>.//
So he let the hare <u>go</u>//and ran <u>af</u>ter the stag.//But the stag could run very, very <u>fast</u>//
and soon it got right a<u>way</u>.//
When the lion <u>saw</u>//that he could not <u>catch</u> the stag,//he <u>said</u>,//'I will go <u>back</u> for the
hare.'//
But when he came to the place where the hare had <u>been</u>,//he found that she had
<u>gone</u>.//'I should have had her for my dinner when I first <u>saw</u> her,'//said the <u>lion</u>. 'I
wanted too <u>much</u>//and now I have <u>no</u>thing.'//

Exercise 27

//I /want to /tell you //how to /get from /<u>Rome</u> //to /<u>Par</u>is. //Either /go by /<u>plane</u> //
which is /<u>quick</u> //but /<u>costs</u> a /lot //<u>or</u> //go in your /own /<u>car</u> //if you <u>have</u> a /car; //or
/travel by /<u>bus,</u> //if you /haven't a /<u>car,</u> //or /don't want to /drive your/<u>self</u>. //I my/<u>self</u>
//like to /see the /<u>coun</u>try when I /travel, //so I /don't go by /<u>air</u> //un/less I'm in a /
<u>hur</u>ry. //I /haven't a /car, //so I /have to /choose the /<u>train</u> //or the /<u>bus</u>. //<u>Most</u> /people,
of /course, //go by /<u>train</u>, //because the i/dea of /going from /one country to a/nother
by /<u>bus</u> //is /still rather /<u>strange</u>. //But /I my/<u>self</u> //usually /go by /<u>bus</u> //when I /don't
/<u>fly</u>. //I have /plenty of /<u>time</u> //on these o/<u>cca</u>sions, //and en/joy /seeing the /village
/<u>streets</u> //and the /<u>life</u> that goes /on //a/long the less im/portant /country /<u>roads</u>. //

Exercise 28

DIALOGUE A

Loue: What do you want to eat, Aini? Would you like some rice?

Aini: Yes, please. And I'd like some vegetables.

Loue: Do you want some potatoes?

Aini: Yes please. What do you have to drink?

Loue: I've got some juice.

DIALOGUE B

Frans: I'm very happy today.

George: Why?

Frans: Because it's Sports Day.

George: Oh yes. Do you like sports?

Frans: Yes, I do. I'm good at sports. Do you like sports?

George: Not much. I'm not very good at them.

Exercise 29

1. You've practised some transcription, haven't you? (=*unsure*)

2. Edinburgh's the capital of Scotland, isn't it? (=*sure*)

3. They think intonation is a difficult area, don't they? (=*sure*)

4. This is a real question, isn't it? (=*unsure*)

5. We've covered a lot of phonology here, haven't we? (=*sure*)

6. You understand it a bit better now, don't you? (=*unsure*)

PART TWO
Phonology in Context

THIS section recycles some of the concepts already introduced and examines them in greater depth. It is particularly concerned with phonological features above the level of the individual phoneme and their function in discourse.

Discourse involves looking at the context in which utterances take place and examining the ways in which speakers negotiate meaning during interactions. Changes in individual phonemes will be less important as meaning at this level can usually be retrieved from the surrounding context. For example, if the 'th' is replaced by 'z' in 'mother and father', there may be a momentary hiccup but the meaning is quickly retrieved and no serious breakdown occurs. Fossilised 'errors' of this type are commonly regarded as having an 'irritation factor' but do not affect overall intelligibility (Acton 1991).

At the level of word stress, the stress placement on an individual lexical item is fixed and cannot be altered to indicate changes in meanings (apart from the discrete group of two-syllable nouns and verbs of the ''contrast' / 'con'trast' variety). Therefore word stress is not a flexible system which can be altered to reflect changes in speaker's intent.

In fact, it is at the level of the build up of the stress in the utterance, the rhythm, that the investigator comes to grips with the range of possible patterns at the disposal of the speaker which may be employed in different ways to indicate changes in meaning. For example, it has been mentioned already that the structural items are normally used in their unstressed form. However, a possibility which is open to the speaker is to use the strong version for special purposes. For example: 'How's your son?' (Where the implication is: 'we have already discussed my son and he is well'.) The same holds true for the contracted forms of the verbs: 'They're coming tomorrow' (expected) as opposed to: 'They are coming tomorrow' (confirmation).

Possible implications of changes in the main focus have already been addressed, and it is clear that context and appropriateness is all-important in determining the location of the most significant item in sentences such as:

> She always goes to the shops on a <u>Thurs</u>day
> She <u>al</u>ways goes to the shops on a Thursday   or
> She always goes to the <u>shops</u> on a Thursday

The speaker will automatically highlight the most important item in his message to cue correct interpretation for his listener. It is true to say that the amount of stress or emphasis a word is given in an utterance depends on its relative importance for conveying the speaker's meaning.

At the level of intonation, context will determine not only the location of the main pitch movement but also its direction. For example, at a simple level, if the utterance is incomplete, the speaker signals this by using a low rising ('listing') intonation pattern. Turn-taking clues are frequently signalled by intonation. For example, if the speaker requires a response from his listener, the high rising pitch is needed in a question tag:

You're Egyptian, aren't you?

As opposed to the confirming pattern:

You're Egyptian, aren't you?

which signifies prior knowledge and is checking a fact already believed to be correct. An obvious use of intonation as a turn-taking clue is the use of the falling pitch at the end of the interaction, usually accompanied by low pitch height. This is called 'low termination' and is a signal that the speaker's contribution is finished and he is handing over the turn to another interlocutor.

Choice of pitch movements can also give the listener insights into the role played by speakers during a conversation. A high proportion of high falling pitch movements would indicate an authoritative figure who is 'telling' or 'proclaiming' certain facts to his audience whereas low rises might indicate an effort to be polite, even deferential. The doubtful pitch which indicates reservation (well∿ maybe∿ He could do, but ∿...) will tell the listener that the speaker is uneasy about the points he is making. This involves consideration of the speaker's attitude, and is another clue which needs to be interpreted correctly by the listener for successful interaction to take place.

Another variable at the disposal of the speaker is the significant use of pitch height or 'key'. The implications carried by use of different keys can be simply illustrated by this example.

Here's 10p	Thanks
	(not a lot ∴ low key)
Here's £1	Thanks
	(more interested ∴ mid key)
Here's £10	Thanks
	(very much indeed ∴ high key)

High key carries implications of interest and involvement or any feelings which are strongly expressed, whereas low key suggests an aside, a restatement of what is known already or lack of involvement. These additional clues need to be noted and interpreted by the listener when a speaker deviates from his expected neutral mid-key.

These aspects of intonation operate above the lexical and structural level. Complex combinations of variables determine how and why certain intonation patterns should be used and these depend upon context, the relationship between the speakers, their attitudes, and the intended and received meaning. Unlike word stress or phoneme discrimination, there are not always clear rules which determine precisely how intonation patterns should be used and consequently analysts feel they lack a systematic basis for description. Most of us acquire patterning unconsciously through exposure to native speakers. Foreign learners who lack regular exposure to the language need strategies which will help them to recognise and produce a satisfactory communicative model. This will help both to improve their spoken fluency and to guide them through the sequencing of ideas in spoken discourse. It will also help them to recognise additional ways of signalling grammatical structure and meaning. In order to prepare them to handle the language independently, the teacher needs to sensitise learners to the meaningful distinctions carried by intonation by providing focused practice and authentic contexts for recognition and production. It is our remit as describers of the language to try to make the rules more accessible and to simplify what is an exceedingly complex aspect of the language.

Levels of Meaning

The Rhythm Package

As seen in Part 1, connected speech is characterised by grouping into clearly perceptible beats which build up to form the rhythm. In the case of English, the rhythm is generally described as belonging to the stress-timed group of languages. Foreign learners who may have no comparable rhythmic pattern in their spoken English do not allow native-speaking listeners to draw on their own linguistic competence and impose a pattern on what they hear. This is serious as rhythm has been shown to be extremely important as an organising principle of speech. As Allen (1985) points out 'speech rhythm functions mainly to organise the information-bearing units into a coherent package thus permitting speech communication to proceed efficiently'. The implication here is that a recognisable rhythm is essential for the native-speaking listener because he needs to recognise and respond to a system which allows him to break up the message into component parts (or feet). If he cannot recognise the natural divisions and groups which are essential clues to speaker's meaning, intelligibility breaks down (Brown 1977:42-55). It can therefore be argued that correct rhythm is an essential ingredient for understanding and as such, it demands close investigation and adequate practice.

Highlighting

As mentioned earlier, a prerequisite to successful control of the rhythm is an ability to recognise and respond to the carriers of the rhythm – the stressed syllables. Our task as describers of the language is to identify the stresses and thereafter to examine what happens in the unstressed syllables.

The rhythm of English relies on a clear distinction being made between the stressed and the weakened syllables. The stresses usually occur on the stressed syllables of the content words (the lexical items such as the main verbs, adjectives and nouns). Notice that word stress needs to be observed in a sentence such as: "'Under 'matters a'rising, we will a'ssess some 'previous 'student evalu'ations". This may also be written as: "UNder MAtters aRIsing, we will aSSESS some PREvious STUdent evaluATions" if the teacher wishes to draw particular attention to the location of the stressed syllables.

Whereas a small line before and above the stressed syllable is the usual convention for marking word stress, a slash before the stressed syllable is used to mark the build-up of the stressed syllables in connected speech – the rhythm. This helps us to recognise the unit of rhythm – the foot.

/Under /matters a/rising we will a/ssess some /previous /student evalu/ations.

The foot starts with a stressed syllable and contains all the following syllables up to the next beat (or stress):

/Under /matters a/rising
FOOT   FOOT   FOOT

Once the learner recognises the position of the stress, he becomes aware of the unit which acts like a bar of music. In this way, the language groups the stressed and the weakened syllables into rhythmic units.

There are implications here for listening skills because words run together in connected speech and listeners may have problems in locating word-boundaries (especially if the foot boundary cuts across a word);

The sun began to shine as he arrived
The /sunbe /ganto /shineas hea /rrived

Processing real speech is consequently quite difficult unless the learner has been exposed to the language over a period and has had the chance to build up good listening skills.

As already mentioned in Part 1, the general rule is that most nouns, verbs, adverbs and adjectives in English will be stressed because they provide important information about speaker's meaning. Listen to the tape and apply this rule in the following exercise.

Now do Exercises 30 and 31

Exercise 30

Mark the following sentences using a slash before the stressed syllables

e.g.   /National Inde/pendence /Day is the e/leventh of No/vember in An/gola.

1.   He has recently returned from a study visit to further educational institutions in Japan.

2.   It will be possible to provide accommodation in the university hostels in the capital.

3.   They undertook to explore the availability of teachers prepared to attend an in-service course.

4.   The Careers Adviser at the Institute has recommended that all of the graduates receive a bonus at the end of the year.

If you are having difficulty with marking, return to Part 1 p 28.

Exercise 31

Listen to the recording of 'The Weather Forecast' and mark the rhythm. Remember to observe the word stress rules

e.g.   'The / fog is /gradually /spreading /eastward. Visi/bility will be...'

The fog is gradually spreading eastward. Visibility will be poor, and motorists have been warned that conditions are very bad. Later, the fog will slowly lift and it may clear before morning.

In the south, there will be widespread frost at first and again in the evening. In the afternoon, however, temperatures will be generally a little higher than today's, and the wind will be light.

Having rediscovered what happens to the content words, we now turn to look at how the speaker 'backgrounds' items of lesser importance for successful transfer of the message.

Backgrounding

In contrast to the stress given to the content words, the structural items are usually weakened. It is likely that all prepositions, conjunctions, pronouns and articles will occur in their weak forms unless they are used sentence-finally or for special emphasis. (For a list of weak forms with their strong equivalent see Roach 1983 Chapter 12).

The /ə/ vowel is the most commonly occurring phoneme in English and students must learn to interpret its meanings from context. For example /ə/ can function as 'a', 'are', 'or' or even 'her' depending on the environment:

> Pass me ə pen please
> When ə they coming?
> Five ə six
> Tell ə to come – // telətə /kʌm//

Here is a short passage which illustrates the wide occurrence of the weakened vowel:

> Thə north wind ənd thə sun wə disputing which wəs the strongə when ə travəllə came əlong wrapped in ə warm cloak. They əgreed thət thə one who first səcceeded in making thə travəllə take his cloak off shəd be cənsidered strongə thən the othə.

Now do Exercise 32

Exercise 32

Write 'ə' above all the positions where it occurs in the following sentences:

               ə   ə   ə ə   ə

e.g.   The teacher sent her apologies

1. The doctor arrived at the door of the hospital.

2. Suddenly, there was a flash of lightening and a roar of thunder.

3. Aesop wrote a story about a fox and a bunch of grapes.

4. The thief was as quiet as a mouse.

5. Some of the class went for a visit to the zoo.

The rule applies *unless:*

    a)   the structural item is located sentence finally:

         who are you looking æt?
         vs
         I'm looking ət John

         What are you going fɔː?
         vs
         I'm going fə my tea

or

    b)   more importantly for present purposes, if the speaker is emphasising a point for contrast or confirmation:

Neutral   soup ə juice?
Emphatic soup ɔː juice? (implication you can have *one*, but not both)

It is important that learners can operate this two-tier system since the use of the stressed version where a native speaker would expect the weak form has the effect of making him wonder why the word has been singled out for special attention. He will conclude that the item is presumably important in the speaker's mind.

Now do Exercise 33

Exercise 33

Write the strong form of the structural words above the item.

e.g.   /hɪm/   /hɜː/
    Tell him, not her.

1. What are they made of?

2. The girls aren't going, but the boys are.

3. Do you think that that looks better?

Generally speaking, the production of the strong versions is not a problem. This is the form which most learners will use naturally and assume to be correct because it reflects the orthography. It takes some time to convince speakers that the correct version is usually the weak one and that its function within discourse is to background the unimportant items so as to throw the meaningful content words into clearer relief.

Contractions

The same principle operates in the production of the contracted forms of the auxiliary verbs, namely, that the normal or expected form is the shortened, weakened version in spoken English (I'd, they're, we've). Learners will encounter these forms in dialogues in course books even at beginner's level and it is important to establish correct habits from the early stages. Notice however that the full version is correct in the written form (I would, they are).

At teacher-training level, it is helpful to require trainees to transcribe the contractions. Transcribe Exercise 34. For practice, Colin Mortimer (1985) has useful dialogues in *Elements of Pronunciation* (Dialogues 102-131).

In each of the above, selection of the weak or strong form will depend upon speaker's meaning. Learners must tune in to any special implications carried by the choice of the emphatic form and look for the intended reasons behind the choice.

Now do Exercise 34

Exercise 34

Listen to the tape and transcribe the following contracted forms:

e.g.   I'd love to go. /aɪd/

1.   They'd all passed the test.

2.   What've you made for lunch?

3.   Isn't that the Bishop's sister?

4.   It'll be their first flight.

5.   What d'you have in mind?

6.   I'll fetch the milk, if you'll find some sugar.

7.   You're always on time, and I'm always late.

8.   They've never admitted it.

9.   Aren't they going to France?

10.   We're the last ones to complain!

Link-up

Another feature of connected speech which affects fluency rather than meaning is the tendency in English to link words together in spoken text. It is not of central importance for present purposes since we are concentrating upon those features which are capable of changing speakers' meaning, but it is of interest to note and important if learners are to avoid a staccato machine-gun presentation.

The two main examples of link-up effects are linking 'r' where orthographic 'r' is replaced at the end of a word before a following vowel:

far: /fɑː/   soldier: /səʊldʒə/
but   *but*
far away: /fɑːr əˈweɪ/   soldier of fortune: /səʊldʒər əv fɔːtʃən/

and consonant -vowel ligatures:

-c v-

right away   walk out   jump in

Now do Exercises 35 and 36

Exercise 35

Look at the following text and notice the ligatures. Remember that we are dealing with sounds here not letters, so although a word may finish with an '-e' in the spelling, it may still be a candidate for link-up.

e.g.   'ore and' 'these areas.'

Mining in General

Malaysian deposits of tin, iron ore and bauxite are now rapidly being exhausted because of mining, and so attempts are being made to discover new deposits.

The most promising section of the mining industry is oil. It is possible that there may be oil under the sea between Sumatra and Peninsular Malaysia; oil and natural gas have already been discovered between Peninsular Malaysia and East Malaysia. Several large oil companies are now boring and searching for oil in these areas.

Now practice identifying ligatures in the following text:

This kind of manufacturing first became important between the First and Second World Wars when there was a shortage of imported manufactured goods; but its greatest expansion was after independence when the government encouraged people in various ways to build new factories. As a result there are today many factories in Malaysia – mainly on special sites of 'industrial estates' built for them. This is the most important kind of manufacturing.

Exercise 36

Look at the transcription of the text below.

Visibility will be poor, and motorists have been warned that conditions are very bad. Later, the fog will slowly lift and it may clear before morning. In the south, there will be widespread frost at first and again in the evening. In the afternoon, however, temperatures will be generally a little higher than today's, and the wind will be light.

/vɪzɪbɪlɪtɪ wɪl bɪ puər ənd məutərɪsts əv bɪn wɔːnd ðət kəndɪʃnz ə verɪ bæd. leɪtə ðə fɒg wɪl sləulɪ lɪft ənd ɪt meɪ klɪə bɪfɔː mɔːnɪŋ. ɪn ðə sauθ, ðə wɪl bɪ waɪdspred frɒst ət fɜːst ən əgen ɪn ðɪ iːvnɪŋ. ɪn ðɪ ɑːftənuːn hauevə temprɪtʃəz wɪl bɪ dʒenərəlɪ ə lɪtl haɪə ðən tədeɪz ənd ðə wɪnd wɪl bɪ laɪt./

Find examples from the text of the following:

1. weak forms
2. link-up -c y-; 'r'-linking
3. dropping of /h/ sentence medially
4. ðə/ðɪ + 'the'
5. deletion   (a)   of /t/ or /d/   (b)   a syllable 'elision'

Summary

Highlighting

- Content words are stressed.

Backgrounding

- Structural items are usually weakened.
- Contractions are usually short and unemphatic.
- Groups of connected speech (feet) cut across word boundaries and there is not always a regular relationship between the written form and the rhythmic group.
- There is a tendency to link words together in spoken text according to certain rules.
- Sometimes phonemes or whole syllables can be omitted in rapid speech:
  next day = /neks deɪ/; Wednesday = /wenzdɪ/.

Look at the section on 'Simplifications in Connected Speech' on page 114. Among the features mentioned above, the most important for teaching purposes will be the identification of the content words.

The Intonation Package

Main Focus

As discussed on page 32, the speaker has a number of options at his disposal when it comes to highlighting the most important item(s) in his message. In the preceding pages, it was observed that all content words will probably be stressed and all structural items of low-information will be backgrounded in order to throw the important items more into relief;

THIS is the **HOUSE** that **JACK BUILT**

/This is the /house that /Jack /built

Decisions as to which particular item among all of the content words is most important for present purposes to reflect speaker's present meaning most accurately will depend on the circumstances – the context. Of all the areas in phonology this is perhaps the most vital feature for both successful transmission and reception of the message. Selection of the main focus item is quickly understood by growing children whose first words reflect an awareness of its central importance for communication ('TEDDY' or 'ALL-GONE' or 'JUICE'). The child selects the most vital item to ensure he acquires whatever he needs. Patterns of language acquisition then develop into the 'two-word stage' where the child selects the main focus plus one other important content word ('DADDY CAR'; 'MUMMY GONE'). The structural items and the inflectionary endings are only gradually added as the child's understanding improves and his control of the spoken medium becomes more sophisticated and refined.

For present purposes, the selection of this main focus can also be regarded as the most crucial for transfer of the adult's meaning. It is the 'Big Apple' in the phonological package and a feature which does not change from one English native-speaking community to another. Australians, Americans and British speakers will all operate this system. As it is so central for understanding, it is worth spending more time investigating this feature in depth.

Perhaps the easiest way to think about selection is to relate it to the concepts of *new* and *given*. The new information will be chosen for extra prominence because it is not known to the listener. The speaker will pinpoint the central word by placing his main pitch movement on that item. Other clues such as increased vowel length and extra loudness also act to ensure recognition of the correct location and some authors prefer the term 'prominence' to cover all of these phonetic clues. However, the main pitch change will be regarded as the most important clue to identification.

Since new information is more likely to come at the end of a unit, or thought group, the probable or neutral placement of main focus will be on the last lexical item:

She wants a new <u>pen</u> .

'wants' – 'new' – 'pen' are all important items but 'pen' is the most crucial concept. It might be helpful to think in terms of major and minor focus with 'pen' major and 'wants' or 'find' acting as minor focal points in the sentence:

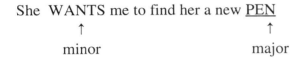

~~She~~ **WANTS** ~~me to~~ **FIND** ~~her a~~ **NEW** <u>**PEN**</u>'
           ↑   ↑   ↗
        possible minor points   major

In fact, the speaker can vary his highlighting in a most sophisticated way by adding or subtracting prominence. (See Brazil, Coulthard and Johns 1980.)

She WANTS me to find her a new <u>PEN</u>
         ↑   ↑
       minor   major

or

She wants me to FIND her a new <u>PEN</u>
                      ↑   ↑
                    minor   major

Most native-speaking listeners are intuitively aware of this system and respond accordingly. However, it is important that teachers and analysers of the language can look at the text objectively and explain the reasons behind these intuitive responses. Just as learners are encouraged to skim written texts to practice reading for gist, they can practise listening to spoken texts to develop their global comprehension.

Now do Exercise 37.

Exercise 37

Listen to the following examples and underline the main focus on the new information at the end of the unit.

e.g.   Consult your new <u>dictionary</u>.

Portuguese is the language spoken in Angola.

The students are arriving from London this evening.

We always enjoy parties at Christmas.

There are several different courses in TEFL available.

Once a concept has been introduced to a conversation, it ceases to be "new" and moves over into the "given" category. This simply means that the idea is understood by participants and consequently no longer needs to be most clearly highlighted. Speakers negotiate the given and new during an interaction and a decision as to where main focus occurs can only be made once the context is provided.

Now do Exercise 38.

Exercise 38

Listen again to the text 'The Weather Forecast' which you have marked for rhythm in Exercise 31. This time listen for the most important item in each unit. Relate placement of main focus to position of main pitch movement.

Underline the most important item in each unit of information. It will sound slightly louder and the pitch will move up or down on the stressed syllable:

e.g.   The /fog is /gradually /spreading <u>east</u>ward. Visi/bility will be <u>poor,</u> and /motorists have been / <u>warned</u> that con/ditions are /very /<u>bad.</u>

Later the fog will slowly lift and it may clear before morning. In the south, there will be widespread frost at first and again in the evening. In the afternoon, however, temperatures will be generally a little higher than today's, and the wind will be light.

Another important rule which governs the placement of the main focus is whether the speaker wishes to contrast, confirm or contradict something which has been said previously. Prominence here will throw the item into high profile so that the listener tunes in to the significance of changing from the expected (or neutral) to the special (or marked) position. The speaker is saying 'pay special attention to this' and the listener is expected to read the clue and to draw the correct conclusions:

> I told him to <u>hurry</u> (neutral)
> vs
> I <u>told</u> him to hurry (marked)

Now do Exercises 39–42

Summary

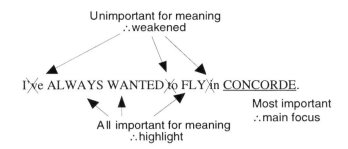

Notice that main focus acts as the central feature in the rhythm package and also fulfils a vital role in the intonation package where it is identified by the fact that it carries the main pitch movement in the group.

Exercise 39

Consider the changes in meaning signalled by the alternative choices in the following example:

    All men are born <u>equal</u> = neutral/expected choice for major focus
       implication: statement of fact or emphasis on the equality
    <u>All</u> men are born equal = marked/special choice
       implication: people throughout the world
    All <u>men</u> are born equal = marked/special choice
       implication: what about the women?
    All men are <u>born</u> equal = marked/special choice
       implication: some work hard and do well in life whereas others waste their chances

Imagine contexts for the following utterances and think about the changes in focus signalled by change in placement:

My husband is not an old <u>bore</u>.
implication:

<u>My</u> husband is not an old bore.
implication:

My <u>hus</u>band is not an old bore.
implication:

My husband is <u>not</u> an old bore.
implication:

Similarly, consider possible alternatives signalled by changes in placement of main stress in the following:

I've always thought she was the cleverer of the two.

The girls in the third year usually play volleyball after school.

Exercise 40

Look at the following sentences and decide how the meaning changes if main focus moves from neutral (end) to marked (an alternative) placement.

1. Jenny has always been my best <u>friend.</u>
   Jenny has <u>al</u>ways been my best friend.
   Jenny has always been <u>my</u> best friend.

2. He went to St. Andrews on Friday to play <u>golf.</u>
   He went to St. <u>An</u>drews on Friday to play golf.
   He went to St. Andrews on <u>Fri</u>day to play golf.

3. All the girls in the second year are required to play <u>net</u>ball.
   <u>All</u> the girls in the second year are required to play netball.
   All the <u>girls </u>in the second year are required to play netball.

Exercise 41

Listen to the difference between positive (p) and negative (n) implications in the following examples.

1. I thought she said she couldn't <u>come</u> (n)
   I <u>thought</u> she said she couldn't come (p)
   (*implication:* confirming a belief).

2. She said she had a sore <u>head</u> (p)
   She <u>said</u> she had a sore head (n)
   (*implication:* but I don't believe her).

3. The reporter said that the play was quite <u>good</u> (p)
   The reporter said that the play was <u>quite</u> good (n)
   (*implication:* but not very good).

Exercise 42

The stimulus is provided. Try to decide how you would respond appropriately using the following sentence:

She usually goes to market on a Friday.

A. 1.   S. Is she going to market on Friday?
   R. Yes, She usually.............

2. S. Where is she going on Friday?
   R. She usually...........

3. S. What day does she usually go to market?
   R. She usually ....

B. I've always thought she was the stronger of the two.

Think of as many possible changes in focus as you can and relate them to the speaker's meaning.

Thought Groups

The spoken language does not have punctuation marks such as the commas or full stops which occur in the written form. In speech we use pauses to break up the stream of sound into understandable chunks for our listeners. These meaningful units are called thought groups (or tone units) as described in Part 1. For analysis on paper, it is usual to delineate thought groups with double lines. There is likely to be a high percentage of agreement about where to pause among native speakers as pausing will be directly related to meaning. Frequently where to pause is a stylistic decision for the speaker. If he is talking rapidly, there will be fewer pauses (and therefore fewer thought groups); however, in a slower, more deliberate presentation where a lot of information needs to be imparted, as in the case of a news bulletin, there will be a higher number of thought groups to allow listeners to process the message:

> //In Northern Ireland //a policeman has been killed //while going to Church with his family.//

Or, alternatively if the speaker is talking more slowly –

> //while going to Church // with his family //

> //The Gas Board//has recently announced//that there will be an increase in charges//starting next month.//

Referring to the tone group (thought group), Halliday (1970:3) would argue that: 'in many cases, in conversational English, it corresponds to a clause, and this can be taken as a basic pattern: one clause is one tone group unless there is good reason for it to be otherwise.' This is a very helpful rule of thumb. Every thought group contains a basic pitch movement. The division of an utterance into a different number of thought groups results in a different number of points of main focus. 'Increasing the number of thought groups also means increasing the number of information points' Guteknecht (1978). The speaker apparently wishes to convey more important information within his utterance than if it were divided into fewer tone units. MacCarthy refers to the tone group as a 'basic structure in the analysis of talk' (1990 p.101) and it is probable that these units have not yet received the recognition they deserve. If they do indeed play such a central role in our grammar of speech, perhaps we should analyse them in greater detail.

The thought group is a clause-length chunk which is a unit of information, or meaning, and a unit of intonation. It carries a significant pitch pattern (or tone) and has an item of main focus (tonic prominence) as its centre point. Viewed in this way, the thought group takes on the same significance in speech as the sentence in the written form as our basic unit of currency in spoken discourse.

Although thought group division is frequently a stylistic consideration, there are some occasions where the position of the pause (the thought-group boundary) may act to differentiate between two possible meanings.

'If you move in quickly switch on the electricity.'

may be understood as:

// If you move in quickly // switch on the electricity. //

or

// If you move in // quickly switch on the electricity. //

Sometimes it is the number of the thought groups which provides clues to differences in meaning. Compare the following two sentences:

// My son // who studies in Glasgow // wishes to become a lawyer. // (My only son)

// My son who studies in Glasgow // wishes to become a lawyer, // (but my son who studies in Aberdeen wants to be an accountant)

Now do Excercises 43–45.

Exercise 43

Listen to the following examples and mark the thought group boundaries:

e.g. a // The old men and women // took to the boats //
     b. // The old men // and women // took to the boats

1. a.   Ann said her mother had gone to the shops.

    b.   Ann said her mother had gone to the shops.

2. a.   The youths who were wearing jeans weren't allowed into the restaurant.

    b.   The youths who were wearing jeans weren't allowed into the restaurant.

3. a.   The king and the queen wearing ceremonial robes stepped out of the carriage.

    b.   The king and the queen wearing ceremonial robes stepped out of the carriage.

4. a.   My husband said Jane is a fool.

    b.   My husband said Jane is a fool.

Exercise 44

Listen to 'The Weather Forecast' and mark the thought group boundaries with double lines.

e.g.   // The fog is gradually spreading eastward. // Visibility will be poor // and motorists have been warned // that conditions are very bad. //

The fog is gradually spreading eastward. Visibility will be poor, and motorists have been warned that conditions are very bad. Later, the fog will slowly lift and it may clear before morning.

In the south, there will be widespread frost at first and again in the evening. In the afternoon, however, temperatures will be generally a little higher than today's, and the wind will be light.

Note: Each unit will contain an item of main focus (and possibly one of minor focus as well):
e.g.   // visi / bility will be poor, //
                      ↑   ↑

        minor   major (+ pitch movement)

Exercise 45

Listen to the story on tape.
1) Mark the rhythm: A /lion /lay a/sleep in the /forest.
2) Add double lines for thought groups: // A /lion //lay a/sleep in the /forest. //
3) Underline the most important item: // A/ lion //lay a/sleep in the forest. //

THE LION AND THE MOUSE

A lion lay asleep in the forest, his great head resting on his paws. A timid little mouse came upon him unexpectedly, and in her fright and haste to escape, ran across the lion's nose. Roused from his nap, the lion laid his huge paw on the tiny creature angrily, meaning to kill her.

'Spare me,' begged the little mouse. 'Please let me go and some day I will surely repay you.'

The lion was much amused to think that a mouse could ever help him, but he was generous and finally let the mouse go.

Some days later, while hunting in the forest, the lion was caught in a trapper's net. Unable to free himself, he filled the forest with his angry roaring. The mouse knew the voice and quickly found the lion struggling in the net. Running to one of the great ropes that bound him, she gnawed it until it gave way, and soon the lion was free.

'You laughed when I said I would repay you,' said the mouse. ' Now you see that even a mouse can help a lion.'

Most native speakers will present 'The Weather Forecast' as shown on page 82. However, notice that various options are open depending on meaning:

'Very bad' or 'very bad'
'May clear' or 'may clear'.

Choice on which item carries the main focus will reflect the speaker's decision based on his meaning.

You should also notice that, although the arrow showing the pitch movement is placed only over the word carrying main focus, the pattern in fact extends over the whole of the rest of the thought group:

and it may clear before morning

In the afternoon however

This means that whichever pitch movement is selected as appropriate by the speaker will start on the most important item *and will continue* to the end of the unit. The pitch movement characterises the entire unit. Pitch movements are studied in more detail in the following Chapter.

Now do Excercise 46.

Exercise 46: News Broadcast

Listen to this text and break it up into pauses (thought groups). Try to decide where the most important item occurs in each. Assume one point of main focus per group:

e.g.   // Finally // the headlines again //

What is the significance of the use of the strong form in the following phrase?

'. . . , but the Coal Board and the Prime Minister . . .'

News Broadcast

Finally, the headlines again.

A Northern Ireland policeman has been shot dead while going to church with his family.

In Zimbabwe, the military clampdown on the Bulawayo area has been lifted.

And tonight's main news: the pit strike is over. Union delegates from the coalfields have voted narrowly to organise a return to work on Tuesday, but Mr Scargill says, 'the fight goes on against pit closures.' He says the union will also press for sacked miners to get their jobs back, but the Coal Board and the Prime Minister both say no to a general amnesty.

Summary

It can be concluded that

a)   The speaker divides the message up into meaningful chunks (thought groups);

b)   each chunk may contain several information-bearing items (content words);

c)   one of the content words will be given special prominence (main focus);

d)   the stressed syllable on the item of main focus will carry the main pitch movement in the unit;

e)   each thought group carries one significant pitch movement (or tone) which starts on the item carrying main focus and continues to the end of the thought group.

All of these parameters may be capable of variation by the speaker to alter the focus of his meaning. However, it is still true to say that most native speakers will probably make the same choices basing their decisions on meaning and context.

Pitch Movements

It has been observed by many authorities from Gumperz (1973) onwards that in conversation with a non-native speaker, English speakers are prepared for lexical and grammatical errors but that mistakes in intonation are not so easily condoned. In fact, the non-native speaker may be regarded as rude or aggressive simply because the intonation patterns unconsciously transferred from the mother tongue are regarded by the listener as reflecting an inappropriate attitude.

The inaccurate articulation of individual phonemes could not lead to such a serious misinterpretation of speaker's intent. The difficulty is that neither speaker nor listener is aware of the cause of the breakdown and both feel at a loss to understand and ill-equipped to retrieve the situation. Intonation is therefore not only an essential feature of a good model of spoken English, it is even more importantly 'the decisive component in the ability to communicate, which is the final aim.' Gutknecht (1978).

If a satisfactory awareness and command of intonational features are prime requisites for successful communication, which aspects of the phonological system are dealt with under the general *intonation-package* heading and how can they be realistically practised and acquired?

In Part 1, a theoretical basis was established in terms of speaker's choices. Two of these have been re-examined in the preceding pages, namely speaker's choice in how he packages his information into meaningful units or thought groups, and how he identifies points of major and minor focus within each group main focus.

We can regard these as 'vocal punctuation' because they help the listener to sequence the information and to process what is most important for meaning.

The third significant choice is appropriate use of pitch movement (or pitch curves) to accompany the text. This is a difficult area to describe even for native speakers of the language who use the appropriate patterns intuitively but may have considerable difficulty in objectifying their impressions and identifying even simple distinctions such as the basic rising versus the falling pitch movements. All authorities, however, agree that this area is of central importance and one which plays a crucial role in the operation of discourse so it is worthwhile persevering.

Descriptions of the uses of pitch movements themselves cause some disagreement among linguists. The following analysis should be read as tentative rather than didactic and as a possible approach which seems to work satisfactorily in practice and reflects native speaker usage. In many ways a more appropriate procedure to adopt would be to work from an analysis of real situations recorded on audio and video tape and to use these to examine what happens in a particular context – to establish a framework for description and to answer questions such as, how do we know that the speaker is enthusiastic/bored? This eliciting approach is the one favoured in an interactive teaching context. However, for present purposes in a written context, it is still possible to define some basic guidelines.

 The secret is to move slowly and lay solid foundations by tackling one aspect at a time. Practice exercises have been provided in Part 1 and it is suggested that even if readers regard themselves as competent in other features of phonology, extra time might be profitably spent on reviewing the basic distinctions already laid out before going on to the next section.

The initial division described by linguists such as Rogerson and Gilbert (1990) has implications as far as turn-taking is concerned. They regard the fall as closed or complete, and the rise as open or unfinished.

FALL   =   ↘   =   CLOSED
RISE   =   ↗   =   OPEN

This means that the basic significance of the falling pitch movement is that the present contribution is complete and it is now the turn of another interlocutor to take up the conversation. The opposite is equally true. The rise (whether high for a question, or low for 'more to come') signals the fact that the context is open-ended. The handing-over to another participant with the high rise is easily explained and typifies yes/no questions in R.P. Think of the *end* of the utterance and whether the direction of the voice continues to go up or whether it falls. This high level ending has already been examined in Part 1 and shall not be revisited.

Low rise

The low rise, as a signal of incompleteness, should be identified and practised also.

Now do Exercises 47 and 48.

Exercise 47

Listen to the 'News Reading' on page 68 and try to decide if the speaker is finished (F), indicated by a falling movement; or un-finished (U), indicated by a low, rising pitch movement.

Exercise 48

Listen to 'The Weather Forecast' again and follow the arrows showing whether the utterance is completed (falling pattern) or if there is more information to come (rising pattern). Each thought group contains one arrow, located over the stressed syllable of the item carrying main focus.

e.g.   The fog is gradually spreading east̲ward. // Visibility will be poor̲ // and motorists have been warn̲ed // that conditions are very bad̲. // Later̲, the fog will slowly lift and it may clear̲ before morning.

Clearly it is important that participants in a conversation are aware of this convention and apply it correctly otherwise there would be regular interruptions and breakdowns in the interaction.

Another use of the low rise is to signify politeness in polite requests as was mentioned in Part 1, page 40.

Please sit down̲

A listener could read the signal wrongly if the speaker used a falling pitch here instead. It would be interpreted as rude and demanding on the part of the speaker. The higher the falls, the more demanding and peremptory the speaker will sound. Obviously appropriateness determines choice: it might be appropriate for the teacher to 'tell' his pupils, whereas a more deferential or encouraging low rise might be expected from a doctor to his patient, where he is anxious to put the patient at his ease. Speaker's choice here reflects his attitude and his role during an interaction and it is clear that this is an example of where misinterpretation might arise if the speaker uses the abrupt 'demand' fall instead of the expected polite low rise.

Now do Exercise 49.

Exercise 49

Listen to one side of the telephone conversation conducted first of all rudely (using falling pitches) and then politely (with a 'smiling' low rising pitch). The second predisposes the listener much more in the favour of the speaker.

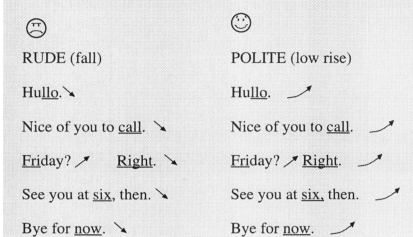

RUDE (fall)

POLITE (low rise)

Hullo. ↘

Hullo. ↗

Nice of you to call. ↘

Nice of you to call. ↗

Friday? ↗   Right. ↘

Friday? ↗ Right. ↗

See you at six, then. ↘

See you at six, then. ↗

Bye for now. ↘

Bye for now. ↗

Intonation is also said to have an attitudinal function which means that the pitch movement selected tells the listener about the way in which the speaker regards the content of his message. For example, it is clear from the accompanying pitch pattern whether the speaker is doubtful or enthusiastic about the information.

☹   There's no harm in asking for it, but. . .

or:

☺   Of course I can!

Each of the above sentences could mean the exact opposite if the pattern were reversed.

☺   Come on! There's no harm in asking for it!

or:

☹   Of course I can, but. . .

This is why it is claimed that the whole meaning of an utterance encompasses not only the lexical items and the structure but also the accompanying pitch pattern selected by the speaker as most appropriate to convey the real flavour of his message.

The 'Doubtful' Fall-Rise

If the speaker has reservations about the information he is giving, it is probable that he will employ this pitch pattern. It carries the implication of doubt, uncertainty and is frequently followed by 'but. . .'

It's all right in <u>sum</u>mer (but I wouldn't fancy going there in winter).

She's very <u>pret</u>ty (but she is not highly intelligent)

The food was <u>tasty</u> (but the service was awful).

A number of researchers relate the choice of fall or fall-rise to the concepts of new (or proclaiming) or given (or referring) Brazil, Coulthard and Johns (1980).

This allows the speaker to change his major weighting to a clause, for example:

// Once I finish this <u>exercise</u> //
(given ∴ referring)

I'm going to the <u>cinema</u> //
(new and proclaiming)

In other words, the central focus is on the new information concerning 'the cinema,' and the end of 'the exercise' is a secondary matter and one which can be mutually 'understood' or 'referred' between the participants.

Clearly the option of changing the weighting is also open to the speaker, depending on what he wishes to highlight:

// Once I finish this <u>exercise</u> //
(proclaiming)

I'm going to the <u>cinema</u> //
(referring)

Now do Exercise 50.

Exercise 50

Listen to the following examples and repeat after the model:

(a) // Mr <u>Mandela</u> // is the head of the A.N.<u>C.</u> //

(b) Mr <u>Mandela</u> // is the head of the A.N.<u>C</u>.

(c) //When you visit the mu<u>seum</u> //you'll see what I <u>mean</u>. //

(d) //When you visit the mu<u>seum</u> //you'll see what I <u>mean</u>. //

Rise-Fall

The falling pitch movement has already been examined as the bearer of statements and 'wh' questions. A variation of the ordinary fall is the rise-fall which says the same thing but with increased commitment. That is why this pitch movement is sometimes categorised as p+ ('proclaiming plus! ') by analysts such as Brazil, Coulthard and Sinclair.

It is open to the speaker whether he makes a straight forward statement or whether he wishes to make the statement, with increased enthusiasm, commitment, surprise or even anger.

non-committal   (☺ = ordinary fall)

enthusiastic   (☺ = rise fall)

It is the difference between:

'I'm going to <u>France</u> tomorrow.'
☺ (statement of fact)

and

'I'm going to <u>France</u> tomorrow!'
☺   (yipee!)

Again it is important for listeners to be able to read signals of this type in order to respond appropriately. An incorrect interpretation of the cues can lead to misunderstanding, irritation and even antagonism on the part of other interlocutors.

Obviously the whole communication process is involved here and the 'exclamation mark' pattern should be reinforced by a smile and a raising of the eyebrows to provide additional visual clues whereas the doubtful pattern would likely be accompanied by a frown. Videos and face-to-face interactions consequently provide vital additional information on which the listener will rely for confirmation that he is interpreting the message correctly.

Drama provides an excellent awareness-raising and teaching context for the attitudinal functions of intonation. It will lead the learner directly into devising strategies to reflect the feelings of the characters. A useful teaching technique would be to play an extract from a drama and to encourage learners to build up their own framework for description using simple terminology. This could lead on to role-plays where learners are required to produce their own versions.

Summary

Analysts have slightly different explanations for speaker's choice of tone.

Halliday			*Brazil, Coulthard*		
statement	=	↘ Fall	p	↘	= proclaiming
question	=	↗ High rise	r+	↗	= referring (+ commitment)
unfinished	=	↗ Low rise	o	↗	= opt out of discourse
reservation	=	↗ Fall-rise	r	↗	= referring
enthusiasm	=	↘↗ Rise-fall	p+	↘↗	= proclaiming (+ commitment)

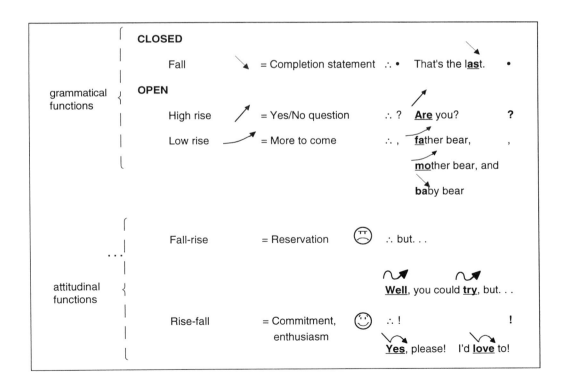

You might find it helpful to think in terms of:

$\searrow$ = .
(statement,
complete)

$\nearrow$ = ?
(Yes / No
question)

$\rightarrow$ = ,
(more to
come)

$\curvearrowright$ = ..., but...
(doubt, reservation)

$\searrow$ = !
(enthusiasm, involvement)

This may be an oversimplification, but it does provide a basic rationale for speaker's choices. Many learners (including native speakers) find this a difficult area to describe objectively. If we can simplify the theory, it is more likely that teachers will feel confident about including this meaningful feature in their programme.

It is important for us to pause at this point and to consider the pedagogical usefulness of these systems. Consider the following:

1. Which system would learners find most helpful and user-friendly (Halliday, Brazil or a simplified version)?
2. Which features would you consider it meaningful to introduce to:
   a) beginners
   b) intermediate
   c) advanced
   d) teacher-trainer level.
3. How much theory would you wish to introduce to learners? (if any!)
4. Which rules would you consider it helpful to give them?

Pitch Height or Key

There is one other crucial variable at the disposal of the speaker, and that concerns choice of pitch height or key. This is the final component in the intonation package:

> THOUGHT GROUPS + MAIN FOCUS + PITCH
> PATTERNS + KEY

From the phonetic point of view, it is true to say that each speaker operates within a pitch range which is comfortable for him or her. The relative height of this pitch band will depend on the frequency of vibration of the vocal cords. Consequently a woman will have a higher and probably a wider pitch band than a man since she has shorter vocal cords, which will vibrate more quickly. Children have very short vocal cords which vibrate rapidly and result in their high-pitched voices. Usually men with longer vocal cords have lower bands and operate within a narrower range than women.

Each of these speaker will have a *phonetically* different set of pitch-realisations:

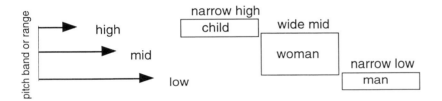

However, *phonemically* the use made of pitch height can carry the same implications for all of these speakers. In the case of the high rise to signal a question form, this will be realised as

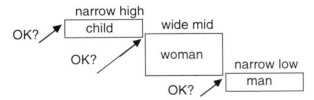

In each of the above, the significance of the high rise is the same (Are you OK?) so we can say that these realisations are phonetically different but phonemically the same. In other words, they each carry the same intonation pattern although the actual pitch heights are different.

Speakers may make use of this variable to add extra meaning to their message. If we look at the falling pitch, this time to express a statement, the expected or neutral way to read a statement would be to use a mid fall:

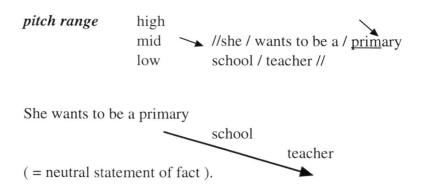

pitch range   high

mid   //she / wants to be a / <u>pri</u>mary

low   school / teacher //

She wants to be a primary

             school

                   teacher

(= neutral statement of fact).

The speaker can either add or withdraw interest from this basic pattern by using a different pitch height or key on which to make the statement. If he says:

     // She wants to be a **pri**mary school teacher. //

using a high fall (or high key), he adds extra interest and involvement to his statement. The implication is that to be a primary school teacher is an exciting possibility and the speaker is enthusiastic about the prospect.

If, on the other hand, the statement is made using a low key

     // She wants to be a **pri**mary school teacher. //

the implication is that the speaker is disappointed. Perhaps there were expectations that she would become a high-flying doctor or politician and, guess what, 'she wants to be a primary school teacher.'

All of these heights are relative but it is surprising how quickly the listener tunes in to a speaker's individual pitch range and can then draw conclusions about whether a topic is highlighted (using high key) or thrown-away (using low key). From the phonological point of view we must tune in to the departures from the expected level and pick up on the significance implied.

Most speech tends to be produced on a mid to low key, with fairly regular departures into high key for special purposes. At the beginning of a new topic, the speaker might start with a high key 'Right!' to alert his listeners to a major new development. Imagine a sports commentator and the way in which speed, volume and pitch height increase as he builds up to 'and it's a <u>goal!</u>'

High key is also more likely to be used at the introduction of a new idea and to be followed by a down drift during the contribution with a low termination ending as a turn taking device to cue the completion of the move. Consequently, in the terminology of Sinclair and Coulthard, opening moves are more likely to contain a high proportion of high key items whereas follow up moves will be produced in a lower key to close the pitch sequence (Brazil, Coulthard and Jones, 1980).

A helpful approach is to regard use of high key as appropriate for something which is unexpected or contrary to listener's expectation:

'They arrived early, but it was <u>closed</u>' (surprise!)

Whereas, low-key could signify an expected outcome or one which does not add more information.

'They arrived late, and it was <u>closed</u>' (of course)

A high key with a broad pitch would convey surprise or incredulity, whereas a low key could signify additional low-information.

A fruitful hunting ground is video observation. Attention could be focused on this area by looking at videos produced for management trainees on communication courses or for enhancing interview techniques which show language use and register to oil social interaction between people whose roles and relationships are clearly defined in terms of status and power.

Now do Exercises 51–53.

Exercise 51

Listen to the following statements and decide whether the item underlined is expected (low key), or unexpected and highlighted (high key).

e.g. She attended the lecture on Rembrandt and it was <u>boring.</u>
(Low key of course. She hates Dutch painting.)

She attended the lecture on Rembrandt and it was <u>boring.</u>
(High key surprised! She usually likes Rembrandt.)

a. I've met Uncle Harvey at last and he's a <u>minister.</u>

b. I've met Uncle Harvey at last and he's a <u>minister.</u>

(Are the rest of the family doctors and lawyers so Uncle Harvey is the odd-man out? *Or* are there lots of clergymen in the family?)

Exercise 52

In the following bits of conversation, you are given a stimulus, an opening cue, and a response you must imagine saying. You are given an indication in brackets of your feeling or attitude. Mark your response in terms of (i) pitch movement and (ii) pitch height (key).

e.g.   Would you like to go to Jamaica on holiday?   Would you like to go to the dentist?

High key: Of <u>course</u> I would!   Low Key: <u>Not</u> a lot
(rise fall, high key, enthusiastic)   (low fall, low key, unenthusiastic.)

1. a: Would you like to go to Alaska?   b: It's rather <u>cold</u>.   (doubtful)

2. a: I've got a parking ticket   b: You're <u>stupid</u> then.   (stating obvious, unsympathetic).

3. a: Why don't you go by plane?   b: Because I can't <u>afford</u> it!   (impatient)

4. a: When do the trains leave?   b: <u>One</u> o'clock, <u>three</u> o'clock, <u>five</u> o'clock. . .   (listing)

5. a: She's been made Head-teacher.   b: <u>Really</u>!   (impressed)

6. a: Are you taking the animals?   b: I might take <u>some</u> of them.   (doubtful, unsure).

7. a: When will you be finished?   b: I've got to do the <u>shopping</u>, and the <u>iron</u>ing and the

                                         <u>cook</u>ing and <u>then</u> I'll be finished.
                                         (more to come, more to come. . . finished).

Exercise 53

As a wrap-up exercise look at the following sentence and consider how you could alter it to convey the feeling or implication listed.

   // She's a very remarkable person. //

1.   An ordinary statement of fact.
2.   'She' is but 'he' isn't.
3.   You are really enthusiastic about her!
4.   Change it into a question. 'Is she?'
5.   Uncertain – She's a very remarkable person, (but I doubt if –)'

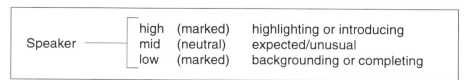

Fig. 19: Meaningful uses of pitch height in English

Answers to Exercises in Part 2

Exercise 30

1. He has /recently re/turned from a /study /visit to /further edu/cational insti/ tutions in Ja/pan.
2. It will be /possible to pro/vide accommo/dation in the uni/versity /hostels in the /capital.
3. They under/took to ex/plore the availa/bility of /teachers pre/pared to a/ttend an in/service /course.
4. The Ca/reers Ad/viser at the /Institute has reco/mmended that /all of the / graduates re/ceive a /bonus at the /end of the /year.

Exercise 31

See answers to Exeercise 38.

Exercise 32

1. The doctor arrived at the door of the hospital.

2. Suddenly, there was a flash of lightening and a roar of thunder.

3. Aesop wrote a story about a fox and a bunch of grapes.

4. The thief was as quiet as a mouse.

5. Some of the class went for a visit to the zoo.

Exercise 33

1. What are they made of?

2. The girls aren't going, but the boys are.

3. Do you think that that looks better?

Exercise 34

1. /ðeɪd/ 2. /wɒtəv/ 3. /ɪznt/ 4. /ɪtl/ 5. /dju/ 6. /aɪl/, /jul/ 7. /jʊə/, /aɪm/ 8. /ðeɪv/ 9. /ɑːnt/ 10. /wɪə/

Exercise 35

This kind of manufacturing first became important during the First and Second World Wars when there was a shortage of imported manufactured goods; but its greatest expansion was after independence when the government encouraged people in various ways to build new factories. As a result there are today many factories in Malaysia – mainly on special sites of 'industrial estates' built for them. This is the most important kind of manufacturing.

Exercise 37

Portuguese is the language spoken in Angola.
The students are arriving from London this evening.
We always enjoy parties at Christmas.
There are several different courses in TEFL available.

Exercise 38

The /fog is /gradually /spreading /eastward. Visi/bility will be /poor, and /motorists have been /warned that con/ditions are /very /bad. /Later, the/fog will /slowly /lift and it /may /clear be/fore /morning. In the /south, there will be /widespread /frost at /first and a/gain in the /evening. In the after/noon, how/ever, /temperatures will be /generally a little /higher than to/day's, and the /wind will be /light.

Exercise 42

1. usually 2. market 3. Friday

Exercise 43

1. a. Ann // said her mother // had gone to the shops.
    b. Ann said her mother // had gone to the shops.
2. a. The youths // who were wearing jeans // weren't allowed into the restaurant.
    b. The youths who were wearing jeans // weren't allowed into the restaurant.
3. a. The king and the queen wearing ceremonial robes // stepped out of the carriage.
    b. The king // and the queen wearing ceremonial robes // stepped out of the carriage.
4. a. My husband said Jane // is a fool.
    b. My husband // said Jane // is a fool.

Exercise 44

The fog is gradually spreading eastward. // Visibility will be poor, // and motorists have been warned // that conditions are very bad. // Later, // the fog will slowly lift // and it may clear before morning. // In the south, // there will be widespread frost at first // and again in the evening. // In the afternoon, however, // temperatures will be generally a little higher than today's, // and the wind will be light. //

Exercise 45

The Lion and the Mouse
A /lion // /lay a/sleep in the /forest, // his /great /head // /resting on his /paws. A /timid /little /mouse // /came u/pon him unex/pectedly, // and in her /fright and /haste to es/cape, // /ran a/cross the /lion's /nose. // /Roused from his /nap, // the /lion /laid his /huge /paw // on the /tiny /creature /angrily, // /meaning to /kill her.

'/Spare me,' // /begged the /little /mouse. // '/Please let me /go and /some /day // I will /surely re/pay you.' //

The /lion was /much a/mused // to /think that a /mouse could /ever /help him, // but he was /generous // and /finally // /let the /mouse /go. //

/Some days /later, // while /hunting in the /forest, // the /lion was /caught in a /trapper's /net. // /Unable to /free him/self, // he /filled the /forest // with his /angry /roaring. // The /mouse /knew the /voice // and /quickly /found the /lion // /struggling in the /net. // /Running to /one of the /great /ropes that /bound him, //she /gnawed it // un/til it gave /way, // and /soon the /lion was /free. //

'You /laughed // when I /said I would re/pay you,' //said the /mouse. //'/Now you /see that /even a /mouse // can /help a /lion.'

Exercise 46: News Broadcast

// <u>Fi</u>nally, // the headlines a<u>gain</u>. //
A Northern Ireland po<u>lice</u>man // has been shot <u>dead</u> // while going to <u>church</u> //
with his <u>family</u>. //
In Zim<u>bab</u>we, // the military <u>clamp</u>down // on the Bula<u>way</u>o area // has been
<u>lift</u>ed. //
And tonight's <u>main</u> news: // the <u>pit</u> strike // is <u>ov</u>er. // Union delegates from
the <u>coal</u>fields // have voted <u>narr</u>owly // to <u>org</u>anise a return to work // on
<u>Tues</u>day, // but Mr <u>Scarg</u>ill says, // 'the fight goes <u>on</u> // against pit
<u>clo</u>sures.' // He says the union will <u>also</u> press // for sacked miners to get their
<u>jobs</u> back, // <u>but</u> // the <u>Coal</u> Board // <u>and</u> the Prime Minister // both say <u>no</u> //
to a general <u>am</u>nesty. //

Exercise 52

1: low fall-rise, 2: mid fall, 3: high fall or high rise-fall, 4: low rises, 5: high rise-fall,
6: low fall-rise, 7: low rises

Exercise 53

1. fall on '<u>per</u>son'

2. main focus on '<u>she</u>'

3. rise-fall on '<u>ve</u>ry' or 're<u>mar</u>kable'

4. high rise on '<u>per</u>son'

5. fall rise on 're<u>mar</u>kable' (but . . .)

PART THREE:
A Workbook in
Phonemic Transcription

THIS section takes the form of a workbook which will build up your skills in recording spoken text. It was originally compiled in response to a request from a group of advanced learners from different language backgrounds. Course members had no experience in transcribing, but felt that it would be a useful analytical tool both to identify areas of weakness in their own spoken model and to keep an on-going record of progress. It is therefore a useful teacher-skill as well as being one which will provide insights into your own pronunciation.

The transcription symbols and conventions used are based on the International Phonetic Alphabet (IPA). No prior knowledge is assumed and the aim is to build up your expertise slowly, allowing opportunities for regular recycling. Short 'Test Yourself' checks will allow you to decide whether you are ready to move ahead to the next section, and answers to both tasks and tests can be found at the back of Part 3 for self-checking. An audio-tape is provided to help to improve your listening skills. This course will sharpen up your skills in auditory discrimination, improve your own accuracy in differentiating between vowel qualities and encourage you to recognise the rhythmic patterning of spoken English. The workbook should be used in tandem with Parts 1 and 2 above.

Before you embark on these 'hands-on' activities, pause to consider why expertise in transcription can be a useful tool for the TEFL teacher, the teacher of the deaf or the advanced learner with a different mother tongue. Briefly:

- It makes you more aware of your own pronunciation because the way you transcribe words will reflect your spoken realisations.

- It focuses on the differences between the spoken and the written forms

  seas
  sees $\Big\} = $ /siːz/
  seize

- It highlights characteristics of connected text and makes you more aware of weakened forms and reductions in spoken English.

- It encourages you to be more analytical of learners' models.

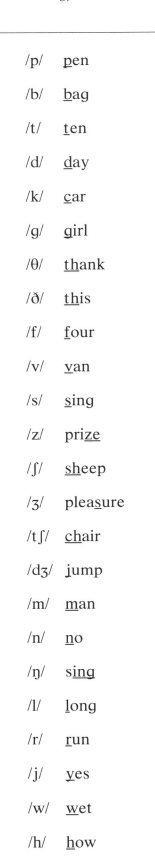

/p/	<u>p</u>en
/b/	<u>b</u>ag
/t/	<u>t</u>en
/d/	<u>d</u>ay
/k/	<u>c</u>ar
/g/	<u>g</u>irl
/θ/	<u>th</u>ank
/ð/	<u>th</u>is
/f/	<u>f</u>our
/v/	<u>v</u>an
/s/	<u>s</u>ing
/z/	pri<u>ze</u>
/ʃ/	<u>sh</u>eep
/ʒ/	plea<u>s</u>ure
/tʃ/	<u>ch</u>air
/dʒ/	<u>j</u>ump
/m/	<u>m</u>an
/n/	<u>n</u>o
/ŋ/	si<u>ng</u>
/l/	<u>l</u>ong
/r/	<u>r</u>un
/j/	<u>y</u>es
/w/	<u>w</u>et
/h/	<u>h</u>ow

Fig. 20: Phonemic transcription –
consonants

- When you look up a dictionary, you will frequently find the pronunciation of a word written in phonemic transcription.

- Most teachers' guides (and even some course books) will contain some transcription as an aid to pronunciation.

The model described is, as always, R.P. for the reasons rehearsed already. You will probably find that your own accent does not correspond completely to 'classic R.P.', especially as far as the vowel qualities are concerned. Look at the lists of key words on page 22. Decide which distinctions you make between vowel pairs and which you do not use. This will help you to clarify your awareness of our own vowel system. For example, in Scotland people do not usually differentiate between /ʊ/ in 'good' and /uː/ in 'food' and in Cockney the same diphthong /au/ would be used in 'go' and 'cow'.

You are now ready to start. Remember to use a pencil and rubber rather than a pen, as you may wish to change your transcription after you have checked the correct version at the end of the Part 3.

Good luck, and remember:

/ˈpræktɪs meɪks ˈpɜːfəkt/

Consonants of R.P.

Many of the consonant symbols are the same as in ordinary orthography so it will not take much effort to master this area. Notice that the symbol representing the *sound* is always written between slanting lines to differentiate it from the orthographic *letter*.

/ p /	pen	/ s /	sing
/ b /	bag	/ z /	zoo
/ t /	ten	/ h /	hen
/ d /	day	/ m /	man
/ k /	car	/ n /	no
/ g /	girl	/ l /	long
/ f /	four	/ r /	run
/ v /	vain	/ j /	yes
		/ w /	wet

Two of the consonant symbols listsed above may cause some difficulty. The letter 'c' may be sounded as /k/ in 'car' but as /s/ in 'cigar'. The sound is always represented, as opposed to the letter; there is no /c/ in the phonemic transcription of English.

The other problem symbol is /j/. This represents the sound at the beginning of 'you' and 'yesterday' and in the cluster /nj/ in 'news'. The symbol /y/ does not exist in English phonology.

Now do Task 1

Task 1

Write the symbols for the first sound in: and for the last sound in:

cigarette   peace

write   peas

know   helped

youth   climbed

There are a number of unusual or exotic symbols used to transcribe spoken English. These are:

/θ/, /ð/

    in 'think' and 'then'

/θ/   is the voiceless sound common in lexical items (thin, three, theatre).

/ð/   is the voiced sound found in structural words (this, these, the).

Now do Task 2

Task 2

Put /θ/ or /ð/ above the correct sound in the following sentences.

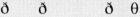

    ð   ð   ð θ

e.g. Then there was the thunder.

(i)   This is the third of the month

(ii)   I thought there were thirty-three of them.

(iii)   They met the other theatre-sister.

/ʃ/, /ʒ/

    in 'ship' and 'pleasure'

/ʃ/   is the voiceless sound usually written as 'sh'. It is found in ship, wishing and fish.

/ʒ/   is the voiced counterpart of /ʃ/. It is found in the middle of the word and at the end in borrowings from French but never at the beginning: 'treasure' and 'beige'.

/tʃ/, /dʒ/

    in 'chip' and 'jam'

/tʃ/   is the voiceless sound usually written as '(t)ch'. It is found in 'cheese', 'matches' and 'watch'.

/dʒ/   is the voiced counterpart of /tʃ/. It occurs in 'jar', 'lodging' and 'badge'.

Now do Task 3

Task 3

Practise using these four symbols /ʃ/ /ʒ/ /tʃ/ and /dʒ/ by writing the correct sound above the letters in the following,

               ʃ   tʃ

e.g.   Fi<u>sh</u> and <u>ch</u>ips.

(i) The <u>ch</u>ildren's first <u>ch</u>oice is <u>s</u>ure to be fi<u>sh</u> and <u>ch</u>ips.

(ii) Be <u>s</u>ure to <u>ch</u>eer if you see the sun <u>sh</u>ining in <u>J</u>anuary.

(iii) At the market, they <u>ch</u>ose some fre<u>sh</u> oran<u>g</u>es, cabba<u>g</u>es and a <u>j</u>ar of <u>j</u>am.

(iv) The lei<u>s</u>ure-centre is the large building behind the <u>ch</u>ur<u>ch</u>.

/ŋ/

    in 'si<u>ng</u>ing'
    This nasal sound is usually written as 'ng'. It is found in 'hu<u>ng</u>ry'
    and 'ri<u>ng</u>'.

Now do Tasks 4 and 5

Task 4

Write /ŋ/ over the words where it is found in the following sentences.

(i)   Please ri<u>ng</u> the bell and bri<u>ng</u> the so<u>ng</u>-sheets for choir.

(ii)   The lo<u>ng</u> road continued windi<u>ng</u> on into the distance.

(iii) They walked alo<u>ng</u> the path si<u>ng</u>i<u>ng</u> and danci<u>ng</u> as they went.

Task 5

Using the short vowel /ɪ/ as in /wɪʃ/ = 'wish', write down the usual spellings for the following words:

/tʃɪp/   /wɪð/

/klɪŋ/   /θrɪlz/

/ʃrɪŋk/   /wɪʃt/

Now transcribe these words, for example 'sing' = /sɪŋ/

ridge   think

myth   ringing

ship   cliff

As a 'wrap-up' exercise, write down the first consonant in the following words:

physics   judge

year   that

cheese

and the final consonant in the words:

climb   long

health   rough

rags

N.B. Remember to think about how to *say* the word and not how to write it.

Vowels of R.P.

Monophthongs

Once learners are fairly comfortable with the use of the consonant symbols, it is time to move on to practise the vowels. Be prepared for more difficulties here as vowel qualities are less simple to explain in terms of articulatory positions, and it may take some patient ear-training to help discriminate between certain pairs of vowels (for example / æ / and / ʌ / in 'cat' and 'cut'). However, remember that English accents vary in their vowel systems and variations at this level are more readily tolerated by listeners than in the case of consonants.

Vowel qualities can only be learnt auditorily, so ear-training is necessary to ensure accurate listening skills as a preliminary to improved production. The aim is to build up the learners' own monitoring system so that they can listen and correct their own pronunciation.

(**Remember** that 'r' is not sounded in words like 'arm' and 'fur' in R.P.)

Long Vowels

Problems often arise because learners shorten the long vowels and consequently these fall in with the nearest short vowel:

      sheep > ship   cart > cut

It is essential to preserve this difference in vowel length otherwise phoneme boundaries fall together.

/iː/   /kiː/ key   /ʃiːp/ sheep   /liːv/ leave

     cheese /tʃiːz/   peas /piːz/
     heats /hiːts/   clean /kliːn/
     heeds /hiːdz/   jeep /dʒiːp/

Now do Task 6

Task 6

Transcribe:

eel   /   /

team   /   /

creep /   /

/ɑː/   /kɑː/ car   /fɑːm/ farm   /lɑːdʒ/ large

laugh /lɑːf/   calf /kɑːf/
bark /bɑːk/   arm /ɑːm/
calm /kɑːm/

Now do Task 7 and 8

Task 7	*Task 8*
Transcribe:	Transcribe the two vowels in phrases:
last / /	fast cars
start / /	calm evening
sharp / /	half reel
	green beans

/ɔː/   /sɔː/ saw   /θɔːt/ thought   /bɔːn/ born

Vary the long vowels:
sharp morning   /ʃɑːp mɔːnɪŋ/
sports scene   /spɔːts siːn/
sea port   /siː pɔːt/
tall corn   /tɔːl kɔːn/
small meal   /smɔːl miːl/

Now do Task 9

Task 9

Transcribe:

last straw

hard steel

bee swarm

taught art

lean arm

/ɜː/   /fɜː/ fur   /wɜːd/ word   /tɜːn/ turn

learning verbs	/lɜːnɪŋ vɜːbz/
early worm	/ɜːlɪ wɜːm/
thirsty girl	/θɜːstɪ gɜːl/
burnt shirt	/bɜːnt ʃɜːt/
stern words	/stɜːn wɜːdz/

/uː/   /tuː/ two   /ʃuː/ shoe   /spuːn/ spoon

Vary the long vowels in phrases:

morning news	/mɔːnɪŋ njuːz/
worst food	/wɜːst fuːd/
cool palms	/kuːl pɑːmz/
first rule	/fɜːst ruːl/
huge shoes	/hjuːdʒ ʃuːz/

Now do Tasks 10–12

Task 10

Transcribe:

torn skirt

first course

horse barn

large firm

Task 11

Now write the usual spelling for the following words:

/fɑːm gɜːlz/

/piːs tɔːks/

/ʃɑːp ʃriːk/

/wɜːld tʃɑːt/

/fɜːst hɔːs/

Task 12

See whether you can work out the meaning of an extended utterance. Although you do not yet know all the symbols, it is easier to read back from transcription.

(i) /fənetɪks ɪz ðə stʌdɪ əv spiːtʃ saundz/

(ii) /ɔːl læŋgwɪdʒɪz juːz saundz prədʒuːst baɪ ðɪ ʌpə rɪspaɪərətərɪ sɪstəm/

Short Vowels

Gradually add the short vowels. Listening practice is provided for pairs which are likely to fall together for learners. For example /iː/ and /ɪ/ – 'leave' /liːv/ and 'live' /lɪv/ – is a problem for Francophone speakers. Minimal pairs will help learners to concentrate on the vowel qualities as the rest of the phonological context is the same. However, do not introduce difficult vocabulary items if you can help it simply because they provide a useful phonemic contrast (e.g. 'big heaps' and 'big hips').

/ɪ/   The first short vowel /ɪ/ has already been introduced during the practice of the consonant symbols. Notice that /ɪ/ is usually represented by 'i' in spelling.

/e/   /red/ red   /sed/ said   /frend/ friend
This sound may cause difficulty if learners speak Arabic, where /e/ and /ɪ/ fall together to /ɪ/; or German, where /e/ and /æ/ fall together. Students in Eastern and Southern Africa and from parts of India may also confuse /e/ and /æ/ in 'bed' and 'bad' since both words tend to be pronounced as 'bed'. It is obvious that auditory discrimination practice needs to concentrate more on those pairs of sounds which produce greater difficulty in differentiation and this in turn is determined by the learner's mother tongue.

/æ/   /mæn/ man   /læmp/ lamp   /hæpɪ/ happy
        /æŋkl/ ankle   /rægz/ rags   /θæŋk/ thank

Now do Task 13

Task 13

Transcribe:

ant / /	lamb / /
shrank / /	cramp / /
stamp / /	

Here are some examples of the first three short vowels:

busy /bɪzɪ/   six hens /sɪks henz /
special /speʃl/   little rabbits /lɪtl ræbɪts/
bank /bæŋk/   English lesson /ɪŋglɪʃ lesn/
ten lambs /ten læmz/

Now do Task 14

Task 14

Transcribe using / ɪ /, / e /, or / æ /

sandwich

red ants

big cat

black pig

many hands

quick dash

Add the long vowels

> black horses /blæk hɔːsɪz/
> four chickens /fɔː tʃɪknz/
> farm eggs /fɑːm egz/

Ensure that the short and long vowels are kept apart:

æ (short)	ɑː (long)
man /mæn/	farm /fɑːm/
match /mætʃ/	cart /kɑːt/
stamp /stæmp/	sharp /ʃɑːp/

Minimal pairs:

/æ/	/ɑː/
cat	cart
pat	part
hat	heart

Now do Task 15

Task 15

Write the correct symbol above the words as indicated.

e.g.   The m**æ**an jumped into the v**æ**an which was p**ɑː**arked beside a l**ɑː**arge b**æ**ank.

The band played jazz, and the dancing started.

The farm cat spat at the lamb and ran off into the barn.

The black landrover was trapped in a traffic-jam at the park.

/ʌ/ /kʌp/ cup /lʌmp/ lump /dʌks/ ducks
     /rʌʃ/ rush /lʌk/ luck /ʃrʌŋk/ shrunk

Remember that there are three 'a'-type sounds:

two short: /æ/ cat   /ʌ/ cut
one long: /ɑː/ cart

and if the speaker changes the vowel, he changes the meaning of the word.

large land bus /lɑːdʒ lænd bʌs/
calm cup match /kɑːm kʌp mætʃ/

Now do Task 16

Task 16
Transcribe:

last lump   fancy art

Sam ran up   land-map

uncles 'n' aunts   hard luck

lovely ankles

Add other short vowels

busy buses /bɪzɪ bʌsɪz/
muddy land /mʌdɪ lænd/
funny hat /fʌnɪ hæt/

Now do Task 17

Task 17
Transcribe:

any action

plenty coffee

lucky mascot

and then long vowels

> spun glass /spʌn glɑːs/
> well learnt /wel lɜːnt/
> dark hut /dɑːk hʌt/
> stuck fast /stʌk fɑːst/

/ɒ/   /sɒŋ/ song   /dɒl/ doll   /ʃɒn/ shone

/hɒt/ hot   /fɒks/ fox   /ʃɒt/ shot

/dɒdʒ/ dodge   /wɒt/ what

Make sure you do not confuse this sound with the nearest long monophthong: /ɔː/

/ɒ/	/ɔː/
shot	short
spot	sport
cot	caught
fox	forks
pot	port

Now do Tasks 18-20

Task 18

Transcribe using /n/ for 'and'

dogs and fawns

short and long

tall story

short socks and long shorts

Task 20

Add the long vowels

stops 'n starts

forty ducklings

busy people

court judge

raw apples

special division

smooth cloth

Task 19

Recycle short vowels

big dogs

spotted cats

jumping frogs

little boxes

black lamb

/ʊ/   /kʊd/ could   /pʊl/ pull   /ʃʊd/ should

Now do Task 21

Task 21

Transcribe:

stood

would

look

foot

boots

Learners have now been introduced to all of the monophthongs in R.P. which occur in stressed syllables, and the next stage is to add the diphthongs.

Diphthongs

There are two sets of diphthongs in R.P. grouped according to the end point of the vowel glide. During the production, the tongue either moves up in the mouth towards a more close position (/eɪ/ or /aɪ/) and this group is called the closing diphthongs.

The second group move towards the central tongue position (/ɪə/ or /eə/), and are therefore called the centring diphthongs.

Closing Diphthongs

/eɪ/: /keɪk/ cake   /treɪn/ train   /ʃeɪd/ shade

/aɪ/: /traɪ/ try   /laɪt/ light   /kraɪm/ crime

/ɔɪ/: /bɔɪ/ boy   /kɔɪl/ coil   /dʒɔɪn/ join

Now do Tasks 22–24.

Task 22

Transcribe:

play safe

late days

main stay

take trains

rain in Spain

Task 23

Transcribe:

night time

tight pile

bright child

my style

white line

Task 24

Transcribe:

boiling oil

spoilt boys

foiled joy

noisy choice

pointed coin

Two diphthongs move up towards /ʊ/:

/aʊ/: /kaʊ/ cow /paʊnd/ pound /laʊndʒ/ lounge

/əʊ/: /ʃəʊ/ show /həʊl/ hole /rəʊz/ rose

Now do Tasks 25–27.

Task 25

Transcribe:

brown cloud

loud shout

down-town

round crown

How now brown cow?

Task 26

Transcribe:

cold toast

blow cold

yellow gold

no-go

night ride

late show

slow climb

quite plain

old toy

high mound

right choice

Task 27

Write the ordinary spelling of the following phrases:

/kwaɪt raɪt/

/braɪt aɪz/

/waɪt gəʊt/

/nəʊ tʃeɪndʒ/

/laʊd nɔɪzɪz/

/naɪt gaʊn/

/ʃeɪdɪd haʊs/

Centring Diphthongs

There are only three phonemes in this set.

/ɪə/: /hɪə/ hear /rɪəlɪ/ really /sɪərɪəs/ serious

/eə/: /tʃeə/ chair /reə/ rare /keəd/ cared

/ʊə/: /pʊə/ poor /tʊə/ tour

N.B. Some R.P. speakers monophthongise this last phoneme and 'sure' becomes /ʃɔː /, 'poor' becomes /pɔː/. This is a widespread alternative.

Now do Tasks 28–30.

Task 28
Transcribe:

real fear   /   /

steer clear /   /

cleared ear /   /

near here   /   /

cheery year /   /

Task 29
Transcribe:

shared pair /   /

rare wear   /   /

fair hair   /   /

spare chair /   /

upstairs   /   /

Task 30
Transcribe:

you're cured /   /

pure fuel   /   /

sure moor   /   /

Task 31

i) Transcribe the following using all of the diphthongs of R.P.

bright area	/	/
mysterious	/	/
here'n there	/	/
pure ice	/	/
shared load	/	/
I'm sure	/	/
great idea	/	/
quite lonely	/	/
golden years	/	/
eyes 'n ears	/	/

ii) Read the following pairs and write down the usual spelling:

e.g. /raɪs/ = rice
/raɪz/ = rise

/fɪəz/	/penz/
/fɪəs/	/pens/
/waɪnd/	/kraʊd/
/wɪnd/	/krəʊd/
/feɪst/	/luːs/
/feɪzd/	/luːz/
/tʊk/	/laɪd/
/tʌk/	/leɪd/
/skeəs/	
/skeəz/	

TEST YOURSELF I

Transcribe:

1.	done	11.	people
2.	sure	12.	repair
3.	want	13.	sinus
4.	girl	14.	journey
5.	shaft	15.	go away
6.	taught	16.	two purses
7.	would	17.	busy women
8.	pearl	18.	Moray House
9.	sheer	19.	one plate
10.	any	20.	too oily

If you have fewer than 15 items wrong over all, move on to the next stage.

e.g.   'any' = three items, i.e. / e̲ n̲ ɪ̲ /

Monophthongs		Diphthongs	
/iː/	b<u>ee</u>	/eɪ/	d<u>ay</u>
/ɪ/	sk<u>i</u>p	/aɪ/	l<u>ie</u>
/e/	b<u>e</u>d	/ɔɪ/	b<u>oy</u>
/æ/	th<u>a</u>nk	/əʊ/	sh<u>ow</u>
/ʌ/	c<u>u</u>p	/aʊ/	h<u>ow</u>
/ɑː/	c<u>ar</u>	/ɪə/	h<u>ere</u>
/ɒ/	d<u>o</u>g	/eə/	th<u>ere</u>
/ɔː/	d<u>oor</u>	/ʊə/	p<u>oor</u>
/ʊ/	b<u>oo</u>k		
/uː/	m<u>oo</u>n		
/ɜː/	<u>ear</u>ly		

Fig. 21: Phonemic transciptions – vowels

Word Stress

Any word of more than one syllable will probably contain a weakened vowel, usually /ə/, but sometimes /ɪ/. The weakened vowel /ə/ never occurs in a stressed syllable.

'father': / fɑː ðə /   'away': / ə weɪ /

       stressed   weakened   weakened   **stressed**

Start with two-syllable words with stress on the first syllable:

'mo ther   / mʌðə /
'bro ther   / brʌðə /
'sa lad   / sæləd /
'an xious   / æŋkʃəs /

and move on to two-syllable words with stress on the second syllable:

a 'gree   / əgriː /
co 'llect   / kəlekt /
o 'ccur   / əkɜː /
su 'cceed   / səksiːd /

Demonstrate the change in vowel quality depending on whether the vowel occurs in the stressed or unstressed position in a word:

'land   / 'lænd /   'Scotland   /'skɒtlənd /
'berry   / 'berɪ /   'gooseberry   / 'guːsbərɪ /
'pose   / 'pəʊz /   'purpose   /'pɜːpəs /

Move on to three-syllable words and allow time for ear-training practice on location of the stressed syllable.

Now do Tasks 32–34.

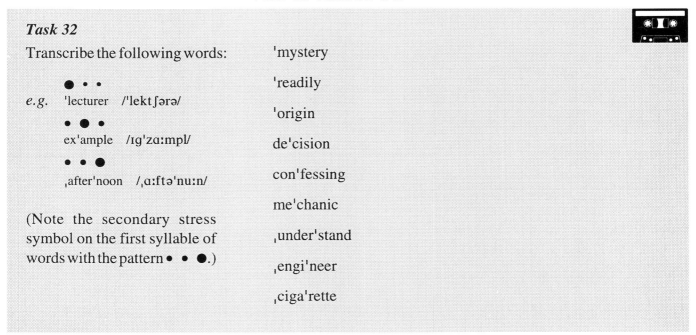

Task 32

Transcribe the following words:

    ● · ·
e.g.   'lecturer   /'lektʃərə/

    · ● ·
    ex'ample   /ɪg'zɑːmpl/

    · · ●
    ˌafter'noon   /ˌɑːftə'nuːn/

(Note the secondary stress symbol on the first syllable of words with the pattern ● · ●.)

'mystery

'readily

'origin

de'cision

con'fessing

me'chanic

ˌunder'stand

ˌengi'neer

ˌciga'rette

Task 33

Transcribe:

'elephant   ˌchimpan'zee

ˌkanga'roo   'crocodile

go'rilla   hy'ena

Task 34

Write down the ordinary spelling of the following words:

/'deɪndʒərəslɪ/   /lɪŋ'gwɪstɪks/

/'kɒmpləkeɪtɪd/   /'ɑːkɪtektʃə/

/ɪks'plænətərɪ/   /ˌfæsɪ'neɪʃn/

/θə'mɒmətə/   /ɪg'zemplɪfaɪ/

/ˌɔːtə'mætɪk/   /ˌæplɪ'keɪʃn/

/ˌpraɪvətaɪ'zeɪʃn/   /kən'temprərɪ/

/'ɔːkwədnəs/   /'kɒnsəkwənsɪz/

/pə'fekʃənɪst/   /'dʒɜːnəlɪzm

/ˌaɪdɪ'ɒlədʒɪ/   /ˌfəʊtə'græfɪk/

/'skwiːməʃ   /ɪˌregjə'lærɪtɪz əv prə'siːdʒə/

/kəˌmjuːnɪ'keɪʃn/   /'pɜːsənl 'sɜːkəmˌstænsɪz/

/ɪnˌθjuːzɪ'æstɪk/   /ə'piːlz kə'mɪtɪ/

/ˌʌnə'fɪʃl/   /ˌækə'demɪk 'dʒʌdʒmənt/

/ə'prəʊtʃɪŋ/

Rhythm and Weak Forms

The /ə/ is also found in the weak forms of the unstressed words in English (the articles, conjunctions, and prepositions):

He blew as hard   as he could
/hɪ bluː əz hɑːd əz ɪ kʊd/

Content words: blew •   hard •   could
weak forms: he •   as •   as •   he
             /hɪ/   /əz/   /əz/   /ɪ/

The weak forms are the usual, unemphatic pronunciation in the middle of a sentence. Awareness of the role played by /ə/ is also important from the listening point of view. Native speaker listeners expect the information bearing words to stand out in the flow of speech, and the low-information words (the structural items) to be weakened by contrast.

backwards and forwards   /bækwədz ən fɔːwədz/
the beginning of the class /ðə bɪgɪnɪŋ əv ðə klɑːs /
tired but happy   /taɪəd bət hæpɪ/
business as usual   /bɪznɪs əz juːʒʊəl/
the first for the prize   /ðə fɜːst fə ðə praɪz/
life at the top   /laɪf ət ðə tɒp/

Notice that there are two possible versions of 'the' and 'to', depending on the context.

'the' + consonant =   / ðə / / ðə kæt /
'the' + vowel =   / ðɪ / / ðɪ aʊl /
'to' + consonant =   / tə / / tə rʌn /
'to' + vowel =   / tʊ / / tʊ æd /

Now do Task 35.

Task 35
Transcribe:

The owl and the pussy cat went to sea.

They wanted to open the door to meet their friends.

Remember to observe the difference between the usual (weak) form and the strong form which occurs sentence finally, or for special emphasis:

/Who are you /looking /at?   I'm /looking at /Ann
/huː ə jə lʊkɪŋ æt/   /aɪm lʊkɪŋ ət æn/

I'd /like /five or /six
/aɪd laɪk faɪv ə sɪks/

You can /have /soup /or /juice [not both]
/jə kən hæv suːp ɔː dʒuːs /

Now do Task 36

Task 36

Transcribe:

What's it made of?

It's made of glass.

What are you going for?

I'm going for tea.

I asked for some.

I've been given some apples.

Where do you come from?

I come from Scotland.

Lists of weak and strong form of structural words can be found in Roach (1983) p 88. This is a difficult area for many learners.

TEST YOURSELF II

If you have fewer than 15 items wrong, move on to the next stage.

1. poor but happy

2. better than e v e r

3. as small as a mouse

4. gone for lunch

5. made to measure

6. the beginning of the end

	strong form (for emphasis, contrast, etc.)	**weak form** (usual)
a; an	/eɪ/ /æn/	/ə/ /ən/ /riːd ə bʊk/ read a book /iːt ən ɔrɪndʒ/ eat an orange
and	/ænd/	/n/ /ən/ or /ənd/ /kʌm ən siː/ come and see /fɪʃ n tʃɪps/ fish and chips
the	/ðɪ/	/ðə/+consonant; /ðɪ/+vowel /ðə kæt/ the cat /ðɪ ænɪməl/ the animal
but	/bʌt/	/bət/ /taɪəd bət hæpɪ/ tired but happy
that	/ðæt/	/ðət/ /ʃɪ sed ðət ʃɪd kʌm/ she said that she'd come
at	/æt/	/ət/ /aɪl miːt jʊ ət tuː/ I'll meet you at two
for	/fɔː/	/fə/ /leɪt fə lʌntʃ/ late for lunch
of	/ɒv/	/əv/ /taɪəd əv weɪtɪŋ/ tired of waiting

Fig. 22: Structural Words

Reading from Phonetic Transcription

Task 37

Here is a piece of connected text. Try to read it first, then check with the written version on page 27.

ðə /nɔːθ /wɪnd ən ðə /sʌn wə dɪs/pjuːtɪŋ /wɪtʃ wəz ðə
/strɒŋə wən ə /trævlə /keɪm ə/lɒŋ /ræpt ɪn ə /wɔːm
/kləʊk. ðeɪ ə/griːd ðət ðə /wʌn huː /fɜːst sək/siːdɪd ɪn
/meɪkɪŋ ðə /trævlə /teɪk ɪz /kləʊk /ɒf ʃəd bɪ kən/sɪdəd
/strɒŋgə ðən ðɪ /ʌðə.

/səʊ ðə /nɔːθ /wɪnd /bluː əz /hɑːd əz ɪ /kʊd bət ðə /mɔː hɪ
/bluː ðə /mɔː /kləʊslɪ dɪd ðə /trævlə /fəʊld ɪz /kləʊk
ə/raʊnd ɪm tɪl ət /lɑːst ðə /nɔːθ /wɪnd geɪv /ʌp ðɪ
ə/tempt. /ðen ðə /sʌn /ʃɒn aʊt /wɔːmlɪ ən ɪ/miːdjətlɪ ðə
/trævlə tʊk /ɒf ɪz /kləʊk.

ən /səʊ ðə /nɔːθ /wɪnd wəz ə/blaɪdʒd tə kən/fes ðət ðə
/sʌn wəz ðə /strɒŋgər əv ðə /tuː.

Contractions

Contracted forms of the verbs are normally weakened in spoken English:

I'll /aɪl/   they've /ðeɪv/

It is important to remember that these unemphatic forms are *usual,* the full emphatic form being used for special purposes.

Now do Tasks 38 & 39

Task 38

Transcribe:

Aren't you feeling well?

He hadn't expected it.

They haven't always lived here.

You're the best of friends.

I'll be back presently,.

They're always late!

Task 39

Read aloud, paying attention to pronunciation:

We pronounce	**I'm**	to rhyme with	**time**
We pronounce	**you're**	to rhyme with	**sure**
We pronounce	**he's**	to rhyme with	**please**
We pronounce	**it's**	to rhyme with	**sits**
We pronounce	**we're**	to rhyme with	**here**
We pronounce	**they're**	to rhyme with	**care**
We pronounce	**I'll**	to rhyme with	**mile**
We pronounce	**he'll**	to rhyme with	**feel**
We pronounce	**they'll**	to rhyme with	**fail**
We pronounce	**I've**	to rhyme with	**five**
We pronounce	**we've**	to rhyme with	**leave**
We pronounce	**they've**	to rhyme with	**brave**
We pronounce	**there's**	to rhyme with	**cares**
We pronounce	**that's**	to rhyme with	**hats**

TEST YOURSELF III

Transcribe:

1.   thoroughly

2.   business as usual

3.   Wednesday morning

4.   what's wrong?

5.   icy roads

6.   self-conscious

7.   ladies and gentlemen

8.   Happy Christmas

9.   government policy

10. see you at lunch!

If you are coping well (and have less than 15 wrong items) move on to the next stage. Remember that the word 'test' /test/ contains four items, or four phonemes.

Simplifications in Connected Speech

In order to highlight the important content words, the structural items and auxiliary verbs become weakened and swallowed in the stream of speech. Other features may also be observed as examples of how the tongue economises in effort without endangering the successful transfer of the message. These are usual in all languages, and should be noted as characteristics of the spoken form as opposed to the written form.

Elision

Single phonemes are frequently omitted from connected text:

next day	/nekst deɪ/	>	/neks deɪ/
asked	/ɑːskt/	>	/ɑːst/
clothes	/kləʊðz/	>	/kləʊz/
grandfather	/grændfɑːðə/	>	/grænfɑːðə/

Elision tends to affect particularly:

* the alveolar sounds   t / d
* complicated consonant clusters.

Entire weakened syllables may be dropped.

	li-bra-ry		*li-bry*
library	/ˈlaɪbrərɪ/	>	/ˈlaɪbrɪ/
	Wed-nes-day		*Wens-day*
Wednesday	/ˈwednəzdɪ/	>	/ˈwenzdɪ/
	la-bo-ra-to-ry		*la-bo-ra-try*
laboratory	/ləˈbɒrətərɪ/	>	/ləˈbɒrətrɪ/

Assimilation

Sometimes instead of being dropped completely, a consonant may change in order to become more similar to its phonetic environment (either in place, manner or voicing). This process is known as assimilation and is an automatic adjustment rather than a conscious decision on the part of the speaker. Assimilations may occur:

regressively ←:

good girl /gʊd gɜːl/ > /gʊg gɜːl/
                        ←

good boy /gʊd bɔɪ/ > /gʊb bɔɪ/
                  ←

horse shoe /hɔːs ʃuː/ > /hɔːʃ ʃuː/
                  ←

does she /dʌz ʃɪ/ > /dʌʒ ʃɪ/
                ←

or progressively →:

it is > it's /ɪt ɪz/ > /ɪts/
                  →

Linking

Various types of liaison happen during speech, but the most noticeable concerns the use of **/r/**.

Normally, /r/ is omitted word-finally in R.P. (e.g. 'far' / fɑː/). However, where the following word starts with a vowel (e.g. 'away'), the orthographic 'r' is replaced to link the two words more easily: 'far away' becomes / fɑːr əweɪ/. 'Linking - r', as it is called, is usual in speech and so useful that, by analogy, some speakers introduce / r / where it does not occur in the spelling. This is known as 'intrusive r' and is found in phrases such as:

law and order	/lɔː ənd ɔːdə/	> /lɔːr̲ ənd ɔːdə/
vanilla ice	/vənɪlə aɪs/	> /vənɪlər̲ aɪs/

Notice the features of connected speech in the following:

I'd LIKE him to ANswer at ONCE.
/aɪd laɪk ɪm tʊ ɑːnsər ət wʌns/

We mustn't DRINK or SMOKE in the LAB.
/wɪ mʌsn drɪŋk ə sməʊk ɪn ðə læb/

The THIEVES hid PART of their HAUL in an OLD white BAG.
/ðə θiːvz hɪb pɑːt əv ðə hɔːl ɪn ən əʊld waɪp bæg/

We should have been TOLD he was GOing.
/wɪ ʃəd əv bɪn təʊld ɪ wəz gəʊɪŋ/

He WANTS to COME and SEE us at HOME.
/hɪ wɒnts tə kʌm ən siː əs ət həʊm/

Now do Tasks 40–41.

Task 40

Find examples of:

1.   Weak forms of structural words.

2.   Elision – a phoneme or syllable which is omitted.

3.   Assimilation – changing one phoneme to another in a particular context.

4.   Linking 'r' before a word beginning with a vowel.

5.   'to' = /tə/ or /tʊ/. When?

Task 41

Write the following sentences in transcription. Make sure you give the correct weak forms for the words printed in small type.

1.   DON'T forGET to PAY for the TIcket.

2.   READ the BOOK and ANswer the QUEstions at the BACK.

3.   At LAST they aRRIVED in FRONT of the PALace.

4.   PLEASE reMEMber to Open the GATE.

5.   WHICH of his DAUghters is aBOUT to GET MArried?

6.   I've ALways preFERRED Apples to PEARS.

7.   They should have beGUN their aSSIGNment by NOW.

8.   The poLICE reFUSED to aLLOW them to be FREED on BAIL.

9.   The NEXT DAY was the PREsident's BIRTHday.

10.   THINK of an Object beGInning with 'B'.

Notice how one word is linked to the next in connected speech if it ends in a consonant and the following word starts with a vowel:

'Think‿of‿an‿object'

Additional Tasks

The following tasks are intended for learners to work through at their own pace.

Listen to the recording at the same time as you look at the written script so that you remember to use the weak forms correctly. Sometimes there are alternative possibilities at the beginning of a sentence, for example 'but' = /bʌt/ or /bət/ depending on whether it is stressed.

Tasks 43 to 46 also provide an opportunity to mark the rhythm. When you have completed a section, look it up at the back and correct yourself. The more practice you get, the easier you will find it to transcribe accurately.

Task 42: Phonetic Transcription

1   A fool and his money are soon parted.

2.   Too many cooks will spoil the broth.

3.   A stitch in time saves nine.

4.   Never put off till tomorrow what can be done today.

5.   A watched kettle never boils.

6.   Sticks and stones may break my bones, but names can never hurt me.

7.   A bird in the hand is worth two in the bush.

8.   You can take a horse to water, but you can't make him drink.

9.   Curiosity killed the cat.

10.   The grass is always greener on the other side of the fence.

11.   Money is the root of all evil.

12.   One man's meat is another man's poison.

13.   A rolling stone gathers no moss.

14.   Don't count your chickens before they're hatched.

15.   Speech is silver, silence is golden.

16.   A new broom sweeps clean.

17.   Look before you leap.

18.   You can't have your cake and eat it too.

Task 43
THE LION AND THE HARE

Once a lion found a hare. He was just going to eat her when a stag ran by.

'That stag will make me a bigger dinner,' he said.

So he let the hare go and ran after the stag.

But the stag could run very, very fast and soon it got right away.

When the lion saw that he could not catch the stag, he said, 'I will go back for the hare.'

But when he came to the place where the hare had been, he found that she had gone.

'I should have had her for my dinner when I first saw her,' said the lion.

'I wanted too much and now I have nothing.'

Task 44
THE HARE AND THE TORTOISE

A hare was making fun of the tortoise one day for being so slow.

'Do you ever arrive anywhere?' he asked with a mocking laugh.

'Yes,' replied the tortoise, 'and sooner than you think. I'll run you a race and prove it.'

The hare was much amused at the idea of running a race with the tortoise,

but for the fun of the thing he agreed.

The runners started off.

The hare was soon far out of sight, and in order to make the tortoise

appreciate how ridiculous it was for him to try a race with a hare,

he lay down beside the course to take a nap until the tortoise should catch up with him.

The tortoise meanwhile kept going slowly but steadily,

and, after a time, passed the place where the hare was sleeping.

But the hare slept on very peacefully; and when at last he did wake up,

the tortoise was near the goal. The hare now ran his swiftest,

but he could not overtake the tortoise in time.

Task 45
THE DOG AND HIS REFLECTION

A dog, to whom the butcher had thrown a bone,

was hurrying home with his prize as fast as he could go.

As he crossed a narrow footbridge, he happened to look down

and saw himself reflected in the quiet water as if in a mirror.

But the greedy dog thought he saw a real dog

carrying a bone much bigger than his own.

If he had stopped to think, he would have known better.

But instead of thinking, he dropped his bone and sprang

at the dog in the river, only to find himself swimming for his life.

At last he managed to scramble out, and he stood sadly thinking

about the good bone he had lost, he realised what a stupid dog he had been.

Task 46
RATS

They fought the dogs and killed the cats,

And bit the babies in the cradles,

And ate the cheese out of the vats,

And licked the soup from the cook's own ladles,

Split open the kegs of salted sprats,

Made nests inside men's Sunday hats,

And even spoiled the women's chats

By drowning their speaking

With shrieking and squeaking

In fifty different sharps and flats.

Great rats, small rats, lean rats, brawny rats,

Brown rats, black rats, grey rats, tawny rats

Grave old plodders, gay young friskers,

Fathers, mothers, uncles, cousins,

Cocking tails and pricking whiskers,

Families by tens and dozens – –

Brothers, sisters, husbands, wives,

Followed the piper for their lives.

R. Browning.

Answers to Tasks in Part 3

Task 1
/s/ /r/ /n/ / j/
/s/ /z/ /t/ d/

Task 2

(i)   This is <u>the</u> third of <u>the</u> month
    ð   ð θ   ð   θ

(ii)   I <u>th</u>ought <u>there</u> were <u>thirty-three</u> of <u>them</u>.
    θ   ð   θ θ   ð

(iii)   <u>They</u> met <u>the</u> o<u>th</u>er <u>theatre-sister</u>.
    ð   ð ð θ

Task 3

(i)   The <u>ch</u>ildren's first <u>ch</u>oice is <u>s</u>ure to be fi<u>sh</u> and <u>ch</u>ips.
    tʃ   tʃ ʃ   ʃ tʃ

(ii)   Be <u>s</u>ure to <u>ch</u>eer if you see the sun <u>sh</u>ining in <u>J</u>anuary.
    ʃ tʃ   ʃ   dʒ

(iii)   At the market, they <u>ch</u>ose some fre<u>sh</u> oran<u>g</u>es, cabba<u>g</u>es and a <u>j</u>ar of <u>j</u>am.
    tʃ   ʃ dʒ   dʒ   dʒ dʒ

(iv)   The lei<u>s</u>ure-centre is the lar<u>g</u>e building behind the <u>church</u>.
    ʒ   dʒ   tʃ tʃ

Task 4

(i)   Please ri<u>ng</u> the bell and bri<u>ng</u> the so<u>ng</u>-sheets for choir.
    ŋ   ŋ   ŋ

(ii)   The lo<u>ng</u> road continued windi<u>ng</u> on into the distance.
    ŋ   ŋ

(iii)   They walked alo<u>ng</u> the path si<u>ng</u>i<u>ng</u> and danci<u>ng</u> as they went.
    ŋ   ŋ ŋ   ŋ

Task 5
chip, cling, shrink, with, thrills, wished
/rɪdʒ/, /mɪθ/, /ʃɪp/, /θɪŋk/, /rɪŋɪŋ/, /klɪf/
/f/, /j/, /tʃ/, /dʒ/, /ð/
/m/, /θ/, /z/, /ŋ/, /f

Task 6
/iːl/, /tiːm/, /kriːp/

Task 7
/lɑːst/, /stɑːt/, /ʃɑːp/

Task 8
/fɑːst kɑːz/, /kɑːm iːvnɪŋ/, /hɑːf riːl/, /griːn biːnz/

Task 9
/lɑːst strɔː/, /hɑːd stiːl/, /biː swɔːm/, /tɔːt ɑːt/, /liːn ɑːm/

Task 10
/tɔːn skɜːt/, /fɜːst kɔːs/, /hɔːs bɑːn/, /lɑːdʒ fɜːm/

Task 11
farm girls, peace talks, sharp shriek, world chart, first horse

Task 12
(i)   Phonetics is the study of speech sounds.
(ii)   All languages use sounds produced by the upper respiratory system.

Task 13
/ænt/, /fræŋk/, /stæmp/, /læm/, /kræmp/

Task 14
/sændwitʃ/, /red ænts/, /bɪg kæt/, /blæk pɪg/, /menɪ hændz/, /kwɪk dæʃ/

Task 15
                    æ   æ   ɑː   ɑː
(i)   The b<u>a</u>nd played j<u>a</u>zz, and the d<u>a</u>ncing st<u>ar</u>ted.

                    ɑː   æ   æ   æ   æ   ɑː
(ii)   The f<u>ar</u>m c<u>a</u>t sp<u>a</u>t at the l<u>a</u>mb and r<u>a</u>n off into the b<u>ar</u>n.

                    æ   æ   æ   æ   æ   ɑː
(iii)   The bl<u>a</u>ck l<u>a</u>ndrover was tr<u>a</u>pped in a tr<u>a</u>ffic-j<u>a</u>m at the p<u>ar</u>k.

Task 16
/lɑːst lʌmp/, /sæm ræn ʌp/, /ʌŋklz n ɑːnts/, /lʌvlɪ æŋklz/, /fænsɪ ɑːt/, /lænd mæp/, /hɑːd lʌk/

Task 17
/enɪ ækʃn/, /plentɪ kɒfɪ/, /lʌkɪ mæskɒt/

Task 18
/dɒgz n fɔːnz/, /ʃɔːt n lɒŋ/, /tɔːl stɔːrɪ/, /ʃɔːt sɒks n lɒŋ ʃɔːts/

Task 19
/bɪg dɒgz/, /spɒtɪd kæts/, /dʒʌmpɪŋ frɒgz/, /lɪtl bɒksɪz/, blæk læm/,

Task 20
/stɒps n stɑːts/, /fɔːtɪ dʌklɪŋz/, /bɪzɪ piːpl/, /kɔːt dʒʌdʒ/, /rɔː æplz/, /speʃl dɪvɪʒn/, /smuːð klɒθ/

Task 21
/stʊd/, /wʊd/, /lʊk/, /fʊt/, bʊts/

Task 22
/pleɪ seɪf/, /leɪt deɪz/, /meɪn steɪ/, /teɪk treɪnz/, /reɪn ɪn speɪn/

Task 23
/naɪt taɪm/, /taɪt paɪl/, /braɪt tʃaɪld/, /maɪ staɪl/, /waɪt laɪn/

Task 24
/bɔɪlɪŋ ɔɪl/, /spɔɪlt bɔɪz/, /fɔɪld dʒɔɪ/, /nɔɪzɪ tʃɔɪs/, /pɔɪntɪd kɔɪn/

Task 25
/braʊn klaʊd/, /laʊd ʃaʊt/, /daʊn taʊn/, /raʊnd kraʊn/, /haʊ naʊ braʊn kaʊ/

Task 26
/kəʊld təʊst/, /bləʊ kəʊld/, /jeləʊ gəʊld/, /nəʊ gəʊ/, /naɪt raɪd, /leɪt ʃəʊ/, /sləʊ klaɪm/, /kwaɪt pleɪn/, /əʊld tɔɪ/, /haɪ maʊnd/, /raɪt tʃɔɪs/

Task 27
quite right, bright eyes, white goat, no change, loud noises, night gown, shaded house

Task 28

/rɪəl fɪə/, stɪə klɪə/, /klɪəd ɪə/, /nɪə hɪə/, /tʃɪərɪ jɪə/

Task 29

/ʃeəd peə/, /reə weə/, /feə heə/, /speə tʃeə/, /ʌpsteəz/

Task 30

/jʊə kjʊəd/, /pjʊə fjʊəl/, /ʃʊə mʊə/

Task 31

(i)   /braɪt eərɪə/, /mɪstɪərɪəs/, /hɪə n ðeə/, /pjʊə aɪs/, /ʃeəd ləʊd/, /aɪm
       ʃʊə/, /greɪt aɪdɪə/, /kwaɪt ləʊnlɪ/, /gəʊldn jɪəz/, /aɪz n ɪəz/

(ii)   fears/fierce, pens/pence, wind (as in '*wind* up the string')/wind (as in 'the
       north *wind*'), crowd/crowed, faced/phased, loose/lose, took/tuck, lied/laid,
       scarce/scares.

Test Yourself I

1. /dʌn/ 2. /ʃʊə/ 3. /wɒnt/ 4. /gɜːl/ 5. /ʃɑːft/ 6. /tɔːt/ 7. /wʊd/ 8. /pɜːl/
9. /ʃɪə/ 10. /enɪ/ 11. /piːpl/ 12. /rɪpeə/   13. /saɪnɪs/ 14. /dʒɜːnɪ/
15. /geʊ əweɪ/16. /tuː pɜːsɪz/ 17. /bɪzɪ wɪmɪn/ 18. /mʌrɪ haʊs/
19./wʌn pleɪt/ 20. /tuː ɔɪlɪ/

Task 32

/ˈmɪstərɪ/, /ˈredɪlɪ/, /ˈɒrɪdʒɪn/, /dəˈsɪʒn/, /kənˈfesɪŋ/, /məˈkænɪk/, /
ˌʌndəˈstænd/, /ˌendʒəˈnɪə/, /ˌsɪgəˈret/

Task 33

/ˈeləfənt/, /ˌkæŋgəˈruː/, /gəˈrɪlə/, /ˌtʃɪmpənˈziː/, /ˈkrɒkədaɪl/, /haɪˈiːnə/

Task 34

dangerously, complicated, explanatory, thermometer, automatic, privitisation,
awkwardness, perfectionist, ideology, squeemish, communication, enthusiastic,
unofficial, approaching, linguistics, architecture, fascination, exemplify,
application, contemporary, consequences, journalism, photographic,
irregularities of procedure, personal circumstances, appeals committee, academic
judgement

Task 35

/ðɪ aʊl ənd ðə pʊsɪ kæt went tə siː/
/ðeɪ wɒntɪd tʊ əʊpən ðə dɔː tə miːt ðeə frendz/

Task 36

/wɒts ɪt meɪd ɒv/, /ɪts meɪd əv glɑːs/, /wɒt ə jə gəʊɪŋ fɔː/, /aɪm gəʊɪŋ fə
tiː/, /aɪ ɑːskt fə sʌm/, /aɪv bɪn gɪvn səm æplz/, /weə ⌈djə kʌm frɒm/, /aɪ
kʌm frəm skɒtlənd/   ⌊djʊ

Test Yourself II

1. /pʊə bət hæpɪ/ 2. /betə ðən evə/ 3. /əz smɔːl əz ə maʊs/ 4. /gɒn fə lʌntʃ/
5. /meɪd tə meʒə/ 6. /ðə bɪgɪnɪŋ əv ðɪ end/

Task 37

This task is self-contained.

Task 38

/ɑːnt jʊ fiːlɪŋ wel/, /hɪ hædnt ɪkspektɪd ɪt/, /ðeɪ hævnt ɔːlwɪz lɪvd hɪə/,
/jʊə ðə best əv frendz/,/aɪl bɪ bæk prezntlɪ/, /ðeər ɔːlwɪz leɪt/

Task 39

This task is self contained.

Test Yourself III

1. /θʌrəlɪ/, 2. /bɪznɪs əz juːʒʊəl/, 3. /wednzdɪ mɔːnɪŋ/, 4. /wɒts rɒŋ/, 5. /aɪsɪ rəʊdz/, 6. /self kɒnʃes/, 7. /leɪdɪz n dʒentlmən/, 8. /hæpɪ krɪsməs/, 9. /gʌvəmənt pɒlɪsɪ/, 10. /siː jʊ ət lʌntʃ/

Task 40

1. weak forms – /ə/, /ðə/, /ət/
2. elisions – /mʌsn/, /ɪm/
3. assimilations – /hɪb paːt/, /waɪp bæg/
4. linking r – /aːnsər ət/
5. tə + consonant – /tə kʌm/; /tʊ/ + vowel – /tʊ aːnsə/

Task 41

/dəʊnt fəget tə peɪ fə ðə tɪkət/
/riːd ðə bʊk ənd aːnsə ðə kwestʃənz ət ðə bæk/
/ət laːst ðeɪ əraɪvd ɪn frʌnt əv ðə pælɪs/
/pliːz rɪmembə tʊ əʊpən ðə geɪt/
/wɪtʃ əv ɪz dɔːtəz ɪz əbaʊt tə get mærɪd/
/aɪv ɔːlwɪz prəfɜːd æplz tə peəz/
/ðeɪ ʃəd əv bəgʌn ðeər əsaɪnmənt baɪ naʊ/
/ðə pəliːs rəfjuːzd tʊ əlaʊ ðəm tə bɪ friːd ən beɪl/
/ðə neks deɪ wəz ðə prezɪdənts bɜːθdɪ/
/θɪŋk əv ən ɒbdʒəkt bɪgɪnɪŋ wɪð biː/

Task 42

1. /ə fuːl ən(d) ɪz mʌnɪ ə suːn paːtɪd/
2. /tuː menɪ kʊks spɔɪl ðə brɒθ/
3. /ə stɪtʃ ɪn taɪm seɪvz naɪn/
4. /nevə pʊt ɒf tɪl təmɒrəʊ wɒt k(ə)n bɪ dʌn tədeɪ/
5. /ə wɒtʃt ket(ə)l nevə bɔɪlz/
6. /stɪks ən stəʊnz meɪ breɪk maɪ bəʊnz bət neɪmz k(ə)n nevə hɜːt mɪ/
7. /ə bɜːd ɪn ðə hænd ɪz wɜːθ tuː ɪn ðə bʊʃ/
8. /⌈jə k(ə)n liːd ə hɔːs tə wɔːtə ⌈bət ⌈jə kaːnt meɪk ɪm drɪŋk/
    ⌊jʊ   ⌊bʌt ⌊jʊ
9. /kjʊərɪɒsɪtɪ kɪld ðə kæt/
10. /ðə graːs ɪz ɔːlwɪz griːnər ɒn ðɪ ʌðə saɪd əv ðə fens/
11. /mʌnɪ ɪz ðə ruːt əv ɔːl iːvl/
12. /wʌn mænz miːt ɪz ənʌðə mænz pɔɪz(ə)n/
13. /ə rəʊlɪŋ stəʊn gæðəz nəʊ mɒs/
14. /dəʊnt kaʊnt ⌈jɔː tʃɪk(ɪ)nz bɪfɔː ðeə hætʃt/
                   ⌊jə
15. /spiːtʃ ɪz sɪlvə saɪləns ɪz gəʊld(ə)n/
16. /ə njuː bruːm swiːps kliːn/
17. /lʊk bɪfɔː jʊ liːp/
18. /⌈jʊ kaːnt hæv jə keɪk (ə)n iːt ɪt tuː/
    ⌊jə

Task 43

ðə /laɪən ənd ðə /heə
/wʌns ə /laɪən /faʊnd ə /heə. hɪ wəz /dʒʌs(t) /gəʊɪŋ tʊ /iːt (h)ə wen ə /stæg ræn /baɪ.
/ðæt /stæg wɪl /meɪk mɪ ə /bɪgə /dɪnə hɪ /sed.
/səʊ (h)ɪ /let ðə heə /gəʊ ənd /ræn /aːftə ðə /stæg.
bət ðə /stæg kəd /rʌn /verɪ /verɪ /faːst ən(d) /suːn ɪt gɒt /raɪt ə/weɪ.
/wen ðə /laɪən /sɔː ðət ɪ /kʊd nɒt /kætʃ ðə /stæg hɪ /sed aɪ wɪl /gəʊ /bæk fə ðə /heə.
bʌt /wen (h)ɪ /keɪm tə ðə /pleɪs weə ðə /heə həd /biːn hɪ /faʊnd ðət ʃɪ (h)əd /gɒn.
aɪ ʃ(ə)d əv /hæd (h)ə fə maɪ /dɪnə wen aɪ /fɜːst /sɔː (h)ə /sed ðə /laɪən.
aɪ /wɒntɪd /tuː /mʌtʃ ən /naʊ aɪ həv /nʌθɪŋ

Task 44

ðə /heər ən(d) ðə /tɔːtəs

ə /heə wəz /meɪkɪŋ /fʌn əv ə /tɔːtəs wʌn /deɪ fə /biːɪŋ səʊ /sləʊ.

dʊː jʊ /evə ə/raɪv /eniweə hi /ɑːs(k)t wɪð ə /mɒkɪŋ /lɑːf.

/jes rɪp/laɪd ðə /tɔːtəs ən(d) /suːnə ðən jʊ /θɪŋk. aɪl /rʌn jʊ ə /reɪs ən /pruːv
ɪt.

ðə /heə wəz /mʌtʃ ə/mjuːzd ət ðɪ aɪ/dɪər əv /rʌnɪŋ ə /reɪs wɪð ðə /tɔːtəs
bʌt fə ðə /fʌn əv ðə /θɪŋ hi ə/griːd.

ðə /rʌnəz /stɑːtɪd /ɒf.

ðə /heə wəz /suːn /fɑːr aʊt əv /saɪt ənd ɪn /ɔːdə tə /meɪk ðə /tɔːtəs
ə/priː/ʃɪeɪt haʊ rɪ/dɪkjələs ɪt /wɒz fər ɪm tə /traɪ ə /reɪs wɪð ə /heə
hi /leɪ /daʊn bɪ/saɪd ðə /kɔːs tə /teɪk ə /næp ʌn/tɪl ðə /tɔːtəs ʃ(ə)d /kætʃ /ʌp
wɪð ɪm.

ðə /tɔːtəs /miːnwaɪl /kept /gəʊɪŋ /sləʊlɪ bət /stedɪlɪ
/ænd /ɑːftər ə /taɪm /pɑːst ðə /pleɪs weə ðə /heə wəz /sliːpɪŋ.

bʌt ðə /heə slept /ɒn /verɪ /piːsfəlɪ ənd /wen ət /lɑːst ɪ /dɪd weɪk /ʌp
ðə /tɔːtəs wəz /nɪə ðə /gəʊl. ðə /heə naʊ/ ræn ɪz /swɪftɪst
bət ɪ kəd /nɒt əʊvə/teɪk ðə /tɔːtəs ɪn /taɪm.

Task 45

ðə /dɒg ən(d) ɪz rɪ/flekʃ(ə)n

ə /dɒg tə /huːm ðə /butʃər əd /θrəʊn ə /bəʊn
wəz /hʌrɪŋ /həʊm wɪð ɪz /praɪz əz /fɑːst əz ɪ kəd /gəʊ.

/æz ɪ /krɒst ə /nærəʊ /fʊtbrɪdʒ hi /hæp(ə)nd tə /lʊk /daʊn
ən(d) /sɔː (h)ɪm/self rɪ/flektɪd ɪn ðə /kwaɪət /wɔːtər əz /ɪf ɪn ə /mɪrə.

bʌt ðə /griːdɪ /dɒg /θɔːt ɪ /sɔː ə /rɪəl /dɒg
/kærɪŋ ə /bəʊn mʌtʃ /bɪgə ðən ɪz /əʊn.

/ɪf (h)ɪ (h)əd /stɒpt tə /θɪŋk hi wəd əv /nəʊn /betə.

bət ɪn/sted əv /θɪŋkɪŋ hi /drɒpt ɪz /bəʊn ən(d) /spræŋ
ət ðə /dɒg ɪn ðə /rɪvə /əʊnlɪ tə /faɪnd ɪm/self /swɪmɪŋ fər ɪz /laɪf.

ət /lɑːst ɪ /mænɪdʒd tə /skræmb(ə)l /aʊt ⌈ænd /æz ɪ /stʊd /sædlɪ /θɪŋkɪŋ
                                        ⌊ənd

əbaʊt ðə /gʊd /bəʊn (h)ɪ (h)əd /lɒst hɪ /rɪəlaɪzd wɒt ə /stjuːpɪd /dɒg (h)ɪ
(h)əd /biːn.

Task 46

/ræts

ðeɪ /fɔːt ðə /dɒgz ən(d) /kɪld ðə /kæts

ænd /bɪt ðə /beɪbɪz /ɪn ðə /kreɪdlz
⌈ænd /et ðə /tʃiːzɪz /aʊt əv ðə /væts
⌊ənd
⌈ænd /lɪkt ðə /suːp frəm ðə /kʊks əʊn /leɪdlz
⌊ənd

splɪt /əʊp(ə)n ðə /kegz əv /sɔːltɪd /spræts

meɪd /nests ɪn/saɪd menz /sʌndɪ /hæts

ənd /iːv(ə)n /spɔɪld ðə /wɪmɪnz /tʃæts

baɪ /draʊnɪŋ ðeə /spiːkɪŋ

wɪð /ʃriːkɪŋ ən(d) /skwiːkɪŋ

ɪn /fɪftɪ /dɪf(ə)rənt /ʃɑːps ən /flæts

/greɪt ræts /smɔːl ræts /liːn ræts /brɔːnɪ ræts

/braʊn ræts /blæk ræts /greɪ ræts /tɔːnɪ ræts

/greɪv əʊld /plɒdəz /geɪ jʌŋ /frɪskəz

/fɑːðəz /mʌðəz /ʌŋklz /kʌz(ə)nz

/kɒkɪŋ /teɪlz ən /prɪkɪŋ /wɪskəz

/fæmɪlɪz baɪ /tenz ən /dʌz(ə)nz

/brʌðəz /sɪstəz /hʌzbəndz /waɪvz

/fɒləʊd ðə /paɪpə /fɔː ðeə /laɪvz

/ɑː /braʊnɪŋ

PART FOUR:
The Teaching of Pronunciation

THE teaching of pronunciation may be regarded as the *raison d'être* of phonology. Unless teachers can see the application of learning in the classroom situation, phonology remains an interesting linguistic exercise, an appropriate study at university level but with little real relevance for the practising teacher. It is therefore important to exemplify how 'phonology' can be translated into 'the teaching of pronunciation' where it assumes a more practical focus and fulfils a central role in the classroom for learners of all levels.

Aims

First of all it is necessary to establish our aim in teaching as this will help to determine which phonological features should be regarded as priorities. At classroom level, communication is the overall focus and consequently the aim should be one of negotiating the successful transfer of information or, as Kenworthy (1987, p.16) expresses it, our 'pronunciation goal must be comfortable intelligibility'.

We must ensure that the speaker's meaning is clear and there is no breakdown in understanding caused by the oral presentation. At teacher training level, it could be argued that a considerable degree of accuracy is also important as teachers will be the models for generations of learners. This necessitates not only fluency but also accuracy in the spoken model. Aims will therefore relate to the needs of the learners.

For present purposes, however, we shall take intelligibility as our guideline. Selection of features for classroom practice will be guided by the test of successful transfer of meaning. In Parts 1 and 2, the most vital feature for correct transfer was identified as main focus and this required also back-up from content-word identification. At the top of the hierarchy, then, it would seem appropriate to place practice in:

* main focus, and
* rhythm.

Intonation patterns were also identified as playing an important role both as turn-taking devices and as discourse markers, therefore the intonation package should follow the rhythm package as the next in importance taking the criterion of intelligibility as a guideline.

Among the segmental features, consonants are more vital than vowels for word identification. Vowel systems differ regionally among native speakers and consequently we are more tolerant of variations at this level. After all, comparatively few people speak R.P. and the accents of the majority of native speakers are somewhere along the continuum between local accent and the R.P. model. What is more important for each of us as teachers is to be clearer about the sound system of our own accent. A simplistic example from the written form demonstrates how much more we rely upon consonants than vowels to identify a word:

> _ _i_   i_   _ _e   _ou_e   _ _a_   _a_ _   _ui_ _.
> (omitting all consonants)

or

> Th_s   _s   th_   h_ _s_   th_t   J_ck   b_ _lt.
> (omitting all vowels)

In both the written and the spoken form of the language, we rely more on the consonants for successful word identification and therefore consonant errors rank higher in importance than breakdowns between two vowel phonemes.

Within the area of the consonant system, it could be argued that the consonant clusters word-finally are most vital for correct understanding as they carry essential information in the form of inflectional endings such as plurals and tenses (see page 14).

A generalised hierarchy of phonological features in need of classroom practice should therefore work from the most to the least important features for transfer of meaning (see Figure 23).

In addition to overall aims, teachers must take account of the learners' first language as mother tongue interference has been shown to be the strongest factor in determining the learner's spoken model. In their excellent *Learner English*, Swan and Smith provide a comprehensive breakdown of phonological errors according to language background. A contrastive analysis between the mother tongue and the target language will help teachers to select which pairs of vowels to practise or indicate whether word stress may be a problem. If the mother tongue is also a stress-timed language, the production of a satisfactory rhythm should not be a hazard although vowel weakening still poses difficulties for almost all learners of English.

A programme for practice should take account of both considerations, namely:

- how important is this particular feature to ensure intelligibility? and
- is there a likelihood of this being a problem area due to mother tongue interference?

We could define our aim as being to increase the learner's communicative competence by minimising intrusive sounds and patterns from the first language where they impede comprehension and encouraging an authentic and natural spoken model of the language.

A.	**Connected speech**	
(i)	The **Rhythm** package	
	I	**Main Focus**
	II	Rhythm – all content words
	III	Word stress
	IV	Weak forms and contractions
(ii)	The **Intonation** package	
	I	**Main Focus**
	V	Pitch movements
	VI	Key
	VII	Thought Group Division
B.	**Phonemes**	
	VIII	Consonant Clusters
	IX	Single consonants
	X	Vowels

Fig. 23: Priorities for practice

Classroom Techniques

A clear theoretical framework is obviously necessary for the teacher but only a minimum of theory should be introduced at classroom level, and even this minimum should be 'translated' in order to make it palatable for learners. For example, young learners could be told to imitate snakes and bees to produce the voiceless /sss/ – voiced /zzz/ distinction in words such as 'race'/'raise' or 'peace'/'peas' (a problem for German and Scandinavian speakers). Obviously, care must be taken to use only words to practice which are already part of current vocabulary. For example, 'ship' /ɪ/ and 'sheep' /iː/ are good items for early minimal pair practice whereas 'hips' /ɪ/ and 'heaps' /iː/ are not. Arabic learners have difficulty in differentiating between the phonemes /p/ and /b/ as the two do not occur as significant contrasts in their mother tongue. Therefore, the puff of air which follows the production of /p/ should be focused upon by blowing a piece of paper. We have referred to /θ/ as a voiceless dental fricative on p. 9. At classroom level it is more appropriate simply to tell the learner to put their tongue between their teeth and blow.

At the level of rhythm, learners can be asked to clap on the important words and to listen for the beat. The item of main stress will be heard more loudly and the little low-information words can be referred to as being 'swallowed' in the stream of speech. Other useful devices are cue-cards to indicate 'enthusiasm' ☺ or the invisible rubber-band to indicate pitch height (key):

Thank you   vs   Thank you!

The sensitive teacher will be able to select from experience and adapt explanations to suit the level of the learners. As a guideline, it would seem sensible to keep theory to a minimum until the upper intermediate stage where explanations are more likely to help and increase awareness. With young learners and beginners, explanations can cause confusion and lead to a decrease in confidence.

The type of practice to be encouraged will also vary according to the age and ability level of the target groups. For example, a song is an ideal context to sensitise young learners to English rhythm.

If you're / happy and you / know it / clap your / hands.

If you're HAPPY and you KNOW it CLAP your HANDS.

(They can clap to reinforce the beat on the meaningful words.)

On the other hand, a dictionary exercise to look up cognate forms of the same root and discover the word stress would be a pair-work exercise more suitable for upper-intermediate learners.

verb	noun	adjective
'educate	edu'cation	edu'cational

Role-plays are more challenging since they provide scope for practice of the attitudinal functions of intonation and prove ideal for advanced learners especially if they can record performances and use the playback for comment and self/peer evaluation.

Informed teachers will select materials and techniques to suit their own groups bearing in mind the considerations mentioned earlier regarding intelligibility and mother tongue influences and the need to build up good listening skills before expecting satisfactory production skills.

A further consideration must be the desirability of providing practice contexts in line with the requirements of communicative methodology. The teaching of pronunciation must be seen to be linked with the other skill areas so that it fits in with the same overall approach and activities should maximise pupil-pupil interaction to ensure they are learner-centred. An obvious link exists between word stress awareness and the building of vocabulary. Recognition of the full value of the vowel in the stressed syllable (in contrast with vowel-weakening in the ordinary syllables) is an important part of word-identification. For example:

/ 'ɔːdɪnərɪ /   / ɪm'pɔːtənt /   / aɪˌdentɪfɪ'keɪʃən /

Other overt links can be drawn between grammar and pronunciation in the teaching of word-final clusters (an area of great difficulty for learners in Malaya, Hong Kong and Japan). If the final cluster is omitted, /dʒʌmp/ 'jump' has to function for 'to jump', 'he jumps' and 'he jumped' and vital grammatical distinctions are lost. A case can even be made for linking pronunciation with writing; the /eɪ/ phoneme is usually reflected in the spelling by '_ay' (day, play), '_ai_' (rain, mail), '_a_e' (cake, same) and there are many more links of this type.

However, the *best* way to practice pronunciation is to regard it as part of meaningful contextualised practice where problems arise naturally and can be attended to quickly. For example, practice of word stress could be linked to the theme of stamp-collecting where learners have to bring in stamps, discuss country of origin (Ja'pan, Singa'pore, 'India, 'Canada, A'merica, Zim'babwe), look up the capital city – /What's the /capital of Ja/pan? – and then write letters to suggest 'a swap' with another class. This type of activity involves learners in reading, writing, speaking *and* the practice of pronunciation (word stress and rhythm).

Here is a quasi-authentic, meaningful task which is learner-centred. It is aimed at intermediate level learners and ostensibly provides an opportunity for grammar practice of the third person singular present. In addition, the teacher should be aware:

$$\{-S\} \longrightarrow \begin{array}{l} \text{- s (if root is voiceless)} \\ \text{- z (if root is voiced)} \\ \text{- ız (if root ends in a sibilant /ʃ/, /tʃ/)} \end{array}$$

/gets/	/kʊks/	/kliːnz/	/dısaıdz/	/wɒʃız/	/tʃuːzız/
↑	↑	↑	↑	↑	↑
gets	cooks	cleans	decides	washes	chooses

The task involves pair work. Students should work with a partner and find out the roles played by men and women within the family. They should interview at least four families and discuss their findings. The following list is for reference:

Who does these things	**wife/daughter**	**husband/son**

gets up first
does the everyday shopping
cooks the meals
cleans the house
washes up after meals
does the laundry
keeps accounts
chooses and buys new things
 for the house
repairs things in the house
sews and mends
puts the children to bed

The main point to make here is that no new materials are required. The informed teacher will be able to see the potential for practising a phonological feature and will exploit the course book so as to develop awareness and recycle practice.

In this way, the teaching of pronunciation takes its rightful place as part of normal classroom activities. The teacher needs to be armed with:

* a background knowledge of the sound system;
* an awareness of areas of potential difficulty;
* descriptions and explanations which can be easily understood by learners;
* a selection of appropriate techniques and materials for listening and for production;
* opportunities to recycle the learning in a variety of interesting contexts (including exploiting current course-books);
* an understanding of how to take the teaching of pronunciation forward as part of an integrated approach to teaching and learning.

With adult learners, key sentences with a heavy loading of target sounds can help identify areas of difficulty.

Sample Sentences

Vowels in stressed syllables (R.P.)

1   /iː/   K<u>ee</u>p a s<u>ea</u>t for m<u>e</u>, pl<u>ea</u>se.

2   /ɪ/   G<u>i</u>ve him a plate of f<u>i</u>sh and ch<u>i</u>ps.

3   /e/   L<u>e</u>t's s<u>e</u>parate the r<u>e</u>d from the y<u>e</u>llow.

4   /æ/   P<u>a</u>ckages and b<u>a</u>gs should be carried in the v<u>a</u>n.

5   /ɑː/   My f<u>a</u>ther p<u>ar</u>ks his c<u>ar</u> on the gr<u>a</u>ss.

6   /ɒ/   Wh<u>a</u>t a l<u>o</u>ng time it takes to st<u>o</u>p.

7   /ɔː/   L<u>aw</u> and <u>or</u>der cannot be b<u>ough</u>t.

8   /ʊ/   Who p<u>u</u>shed me and st<u>oo</u>d on my f<u>oo</u>t?

9   /uː/   F<u>ew</u> of the gr<u>ou</u>p obey the r<u>u</u>les.

10 /ʌ/   The elephant's t<u>u</u>sks were c<u>o</u>vered with m<u>u</u>d.
*

12 /eɪ/   Will the sh<u>a</u>pe st<u>ay</u> the s<u>a</u>me?

13 /əʊ/   D<u>o</u>n't you kn<u>ow</u> who wr<u>o</u>te it?

14 /aɪ/   Fl<u>y</u> overn<u>i</u>ght if you want to save t<u>i</u>me.

15 /aʊ/   H<u>ow</u> soon can you get <u>ou</u>t of t<u>ow</u>n?

16 /ɔɪ/   The v<u>oi</u>ce of a small b<u>oy</u> can make a loud n<u>oi</u>se.

17 /ɪə/   Try to st<u>eer</u> cl<u>ear</u> of qu<u>eer</u> id<u>ea</u>s.

18 /eə/   F<u>air</u> h<u>air</u> is quite r<u>are</u> in this <u>a</u>rea.

19 /ʊə/   I'm s<u>ure</u> he'll be f<u>ur</u>ious.

* The /ə/ is vowel number 11. It is not included in this list as it *only* occurs in unstressed syllables in English. Its function is discussed on page 20.

With younger learners, key words fulfil the same function as useful reference points.

/iː/ is the long 'ee' in 'sheep'.
Key word: sheep

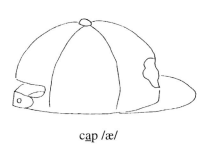

cap /æ/

cow /aʊ/

sheep /iː/

hen /e/

ears /ɪə/

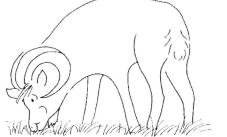

goat /əʊ/

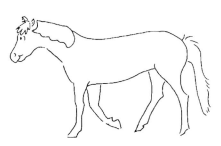

horse /ɔː/

Consonants

1   /p/   Peter's hoping to see your ship.

2   /b/   Is it above the boy's club?

3   /t/   We'd better get a taxi.

4   /d/   My daughter's already in bed.

5   /k/   I've broken the back of the cupboard.

6   /g/   Is the dog in the garden again?

7   /m/   When's your mother coming home?

8   /n/   Have you seen any other notebooks?

9   /ŋ/   Then the bell rang and the singing stopped.

10   /f/   They were far safer on the roof.

11   /v/   Five of them are leaving the village.

12   /θ/   I don't think it's worth anything.

13   /ð/   Is there another place to bathe?

14   /s/   If you pass me the essay I'll sign it.

15   /z/   The boys are too lazy to go to the zoo today.

16   /ʃ/   I buy the fish in the shop near the station.

17   /ʒ/   She usually wears rouge on the stage.

18   /tʃ/   Fetch a chair from the kitchen, please.

19   /dʒ/   I haven't heard George play jazz for ages.

20   /h/   Did Henry behave himself?

21   /r/   Hurry back before the rain starts.

22   /l/   Call for us as early as you like.

23   /w/   We're going away on Wednesday.

24   /j/   Young people seldom see beyond the present.

Activities

The following collection of ideas is selected bearing in mind the points discussed above. As far as possible, the materials are simple and similar to those which teachers would normally encounter in course work. The purpose here is to demonstrate an overt link with the teaching of pronunciation and to encourage teachers to view this area as a natural and central part of acquiring a good model of English – a target usually regarded as a high priority by the learners themselves.

SAMPLE ACTIVITY	*LEVEL*	*PHONOLOGICAL FEATURE*	*METHODOLOGY*
1. A DOG and a CAT	BEGINNERS	*Stress content words and weaken structural items*	building vocabulary
2. Birthdays	LOWER INTERMEDIATE	/θ/	meaningful context to practise problem consonant
3. Poems / Songs		*Rhythm*	fun activity
4. Story in past tense	INTERMEDIATE	'- ed' /- t/ /- d/ /- ɪd/	simple past listening / speaking integrated skills (grammar)
5. Who/When/Where		*Main focus*	Wh- questions Pair work
6. Questionnaire		*Rhythm*	structures 'I can . . . but I can't . . . .'
7. Nationalities		*Intonation in tag questions*	question forms and he's, she's, they're
8. Picture Dominoes	UPPER INTERMEDIATE	æ / e	auditory discrimination accuracy: pair work
9. Word Families		*Word stress*	vocabulary-building dictionary work
10. Role-play	ADVANCED	*Attitudinal functions of intonation and key*	oral skills record and playback for self/peer evaluation

Activity 1: Stress and Rhythm

Level: Beginners.

Methodology: Pair work game.
                  Link to vocabulary building.

Materials: Cue cards

This activity links the learning of the names of animals with practice of content word identification and vowel-weakening in the structural items. It is suitable for young beginners.

At the presentation stage, the teacher holds up a picture of an animal and models the pronunciation:

> a DOG
> /ə dɒg/

She then holds up a second picture and says:

> a DOG and a CAT
> /ə dɒg ənd ə kæt/

Five new items are sufficient – a dog, a cat, a cow, a goat and a sheep. As the teacher holds up the pictures, the children should be told to clap their hands and say the names of the animals more loudly 'so that we can all hear them.'

> a DOG and a CAT and a SHEEP
>   clap   clap   clap

Pair work

Each pair of children is then given a set of cards showing the pictures of the animals (three examples of each) and the cards are laid face-down on the desk. They take it in turns to turn over two cards and they must call out the names of the animals on the cards.

> a SHEEP and a GOAT

If two sheep are turned up at the same time, the child wins the 'trick'. The winner is the one with most tricks.

Cue cards on the following page may be photocopied and enlarged for classroom practice.

Activity 2: Consonant / θ/

Level: Lower–intermediate.

Methodology: Most learners of English have problems with the production of 'th' as this sound does not occur in many languages. / θ / can be meaningfully integrated with practice of structures and dates in talking about the birthdays of children in the class.

Materials: A calendar.

After introducing the months of the year and the days of the week, the teacher can use this context to check on the production of the voiceless dental fricative / θ /. For classroom purposes, it is enough to tell the learners to put their tongue-tip between their teeth and blow to pronounce 'th' correctly.

She starts by telling the children the date of her own birthday.

'My bir<u>th</u>day is on the 28<u>th</u> of January.'

In pairs, the children ask each other the dates of their birthdays and then turn to the next pair and say:

'This is Yvette. Her bir<u>th</u>day is on the <u>3</u>rd of July' or
'This is Jean. His bir<u>th</u>day is on the 26<u>th</u> of April.'

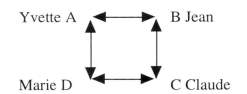

Yvette A   B Jean

Marie D   C Claude

April
M	T	W	T	F	S	S
				1	2	3
4	5	6	7	8	9	10
11	12	13	14	15	16	17
18	19	20	21	22	23	24
25	(26)	27	28	29	30	

Jean's
Birthday

May
M	T	W	T	F	S	S
						1
2	3	4	5	6	7	8
9	10	11	12	13	14	15
16	17	18	19	20	21	22
23	24	25	26	27	28	29
30	31					

June
M	T	W	T	F	S	S
		1	2	3	4	5
6	7	8	9	10	11	12
13	14	15	16	17	18	19
20	21	22	23	24	25	26
27	28	29	30			

July
M	T	W	T	F	S	S
				1	2	(3)
4	5	6	7	8	9	10
11	12	13	14	15	16	17
18	19	20	21	22	23	24
25	26	27	28	29	30	31

Yvette's
Birthday

To practise the voiced / ð /, build up information about members of the children's family, using vocabulary with a heavy-loading of this phoneme:

mo<u>th</u>er
bro<u>th</u>er
fa<u>th</u>er
grandmo<u>th</u>er

Activity 3: Rhythm

Level: Lower – intermediate.

Methodology: Songs and poems provide excellent materials to help learners to feel the beat in the language. They should be encouraged to clap as they sing. In this song, new vocabulary items can be introduced in response to suggestions elicited from the learners themselves.

Materials: Song 'This is the Way'.

All children (and even many adults) enjoy songs especially as a Friday afternoon activity. They also provide excellent source material for recycling structures and extending vocabulary. For present purposes, the function of the song is to reinforce awareness of the rhythm in English.

The teacher plays the song to the learners and mimes each activity. The children clap as they listen to the beat. New words are explained and the teacher encourages learners to suggest more activities and supplies the necessary vocabulary.

The song may be sung as a class, or groups may take it in turns to add a new verse such as:

> THIS is the WAY we WALK to SCHOOL.
> THIS is the WAY we WATCH T.V.
> THIS is the WAY we PLAY OUTSIDE.

Activity 4: Past tense {-ed}

Level: Intermediate

Methodology: Link with grammar (past tense of weak forms)

Materials: Cue cards for the story of "Goldilocks and the Three Bears".

The teacher tells the story of the Three Bears and explains any difficult vocabulary ("porridge", "skipped", "returned").

The past tenses of actions verbs are written up on the blackboard. The teacher is aware of the rule on p. 13 regarding the appropriate phonemic realisations.

-t	-d	-ɪd
skipped	lived	tasted
looked	returned	waited
bumped	smiled	pointed
watched		
walked		
jumped		

The attention of the pupils is drawn to the different sounds at the ends of the words but no rules are necessary at classroom-level.

The pictures have been cut up to form sets of 12 and each group of four children is given a set (in any order). The groups are told to talk about their pictures using the vocabulary on the blackboard and then to put the story into the correct order. Pupils are then asked to write a sentence about each picture. After 15 minutes, the groups are asked to retell the story in the correct order and the class can vote for the most successful presentation.

Cue cards on the following page may be photocopied and enlarged for classroom practice.

Goldilocks and the three bears

name _____

Activity 5: Main Focus

Level: Intermediate.

Methodology: Information transfer task in pairs.

Materials: Question cards and Weather forecasts from local newspapers as an awareness-arousing activity.

The teacher provides a set of cards with names and places of work. She holds up a name in one hand 'LU' and a work-place in the other 'HOSPITAL'. She tells the class:

LU WORKS at the HOSPITAL.

She then models the question and answer:

Who works at the hospital?
Lu works at the hospital.
Where does Lu work?
Lu works at the hospital.

Similarly, she holds up other names and places:

Yang	restaurant
Jiang	office
Jie	factory

and asks the children to respond appropriately stressing the name in response to 'who' and the place in response to 'where'. The teacher must ensure that the learners connect the response with the stimulus word. Extra linguistic gestures such as a nod or a hand-movement will help learners to identify the main focus. She tells the learners to write down sentences about where their mother/father/uncle work and puts on the blackboard:

my UNCLE WORKS at the SCHOOL.

In pairs, children ask each other questions starting with:

Who – ?   and
Where – ?

The teacher walks round ensuring that the main focus is stressed appropriately.

The teacher then produces a weather forecast based on a local newspaper, for example:

Places	*Weather*	*Time*
Ankara	sunny	morning
Istanbul	wet	afternoon
Antalya	cloudy	evening

and models:

> In ANKARA it will be SUNNY in the MORNING.

She then writes it on the blackboard and holds up cue cards.

> WHERE? WHAT? WHEN?

and models again, pointing to the main focus:

(where)	In **ANKARA** it will be SUNNY in the MORNING.
(what)	In ANKARA it will be **SUNNY** in the MORNING.
(when)	In ANKARA it will be SUNNY in the **MORNING.**

The children practise the activity, using the examples of Istanbul and Antalya, changing the main focus in response to the cue cards. The teacher points for visual reinforcement.

Pair work

An information-transfer task can now be devised so that pupils can ask each other about the weather forecast. The class should be divided into pairs, with one partner being given Card A and the other partner Card B. They should then ask one another questions starting:

> Where will it be – ?
> What will it be like in – ?
> When will it be – ?

and answer using full sentences.

Question cards on the following page may be photocopied and enlarged for classroom practice.

Sample Card A

PLACE	WEATHER	TIME
Dusseldorf	–	early morning
Hamburg	fine	–
Berlin	cloudy	–
–	drizzle	early afternoon
Frankfurt	–	late afternoon
Dresden	warm	–
–	thunder	later this evening
Hanover	snow	–

Sample Card B

PLACE	WEATHER	TIME
Dusseldorf	wet	–
–	fine	late morning
Berlin	–	midday
Tubingen	drizzle	–
Frankfurt	sunny	–
–	warm	early evening
Bonn	thunder	–
–	snow	tonight

143

Where

What

When

Activity 6: Rhythm and Contracted Forms.

Level: Intermediate.

Methodology: Learner-learner interactions are maximised by filling in a questionnaire about sports. This activity also recycles practice of the structures 'I can – ' and 'I can't – '.

Materials: Questionnaire.

The teacher talks to the pupils about the sports they play and suggests they should find out which sport is the most popular in their class. She models:

    'I can swim but I can't play golf' –
    'I can SWIM but I CAN'T PLAY GOLF'.

She then asks two children questions and puts their responses up on the blackboard, for example:

    MARY can PLAY TENNIS but she CAN'T SKI.

New vocabulary is explained and possible additional sports discussed.

Group work

Each child is given a questionnaire (example below) and must fill in the names of their friends along the top of the columns. They fill in the column headed 'you'. If the class is small, pupils may move around to question their friends and tick the columns. If the numbers are large, they can form into smaller groups with each group reporting back on their favourite sport at the end of the activity.

Pupils should make up sentences using this pattern:

    MARY can SWIM, but she CAN'T SKI

    JOHN can – , but he CAN'T –

SPORT	YOU	Mary									
swim	✓	✓									
tennis	—	✓									
fish	—	—									
football	—	—									
ski	—	—									
jog	✓	✓									
cycle	✓	✓									
Jump 1 m.	✓	—									

Sample Questionnaire

Activity 7: Intonation in Tag Questions

Level:　　　　　Intermediate.

Methodology:　　This focused practice on intonation patterns in tag questions links in with grammatical structures such as 'He's from – ' 'They're from – '.

Materials:　　　Cue cards of different nationalities.

In conversation it is important to interpret the signals about a speaker's meaning correctly. Two different patterns are used in tag questions to tell the listener whether a speaker is fairly sure about a fact and is just seeking agreement:

　　　　You're from **France, are**n't you?
　　　　(= fairly sure, not a real question).

or is genuinely in need of an answer because he is unsure himself:

　　　　You're from **France, are**n't you?

The teacher holds up a cue-card where the nationality of the character is clear and models:

　　　　He's from **China, isn't** he?

nodding and looking confident. She then holds up another cue-card looking doubtful, and models

　　　　He's from **Rus**sia, **is**n't he?

She elicits the rule from the learners that if one is sure, the voice falls at the end and if one is not sure the voice goes up to indicate a question. The structures are written on the blackboard.

She then models other examples such as 'They're from Ja**pan, are**n't they?' and asks the learners to say 'Yes, sure' or 'No, not sure' so that they link the pitch movement to speaker's meaning.

Pair work

Cards of different nationalities are then handed out and the learners must respond appropriately to questions, using the grammatical forms on the blackboard. The response can be reinforced by thumbs-up for 'sure' and thumbs-down for 'unsure'. The purpose is to help learners to internalise the meaning behind speaker's choice of intonation pattern.

Cue cards on the following page may be photocopied and enlarged for classroom practice.

Activity 8: Vowels /e/, /æ/

Level: Intermediate.

Methodology: An accuracy-based task to aid auditory discrimination.
Listening precedes production.

Materials: Sets of picture domino cards with items containing /e/ and /æ/

Following focused practice (such as minimal pairs), the teacher tells the learners that they are going to play a game where they must link the words with the same vowel sound together. (All the words must be in their vocabulary already). She holds up an enlarged card with a c**a**t and another with a l**a**mp and places them together.

She then asks a child to find a picture of an object with the / e / sounds as in 'bell'. They play a game of picture-dominoes, saying the words as they fit them together.

In pairs, the children are given sets of cards (five each) and they must play the game to see who is the first to be left without any more cards.

Similar games can be devised using /iː / 'sheep' and /ɪ/ 'ship', or /æ/ 'cat' and /ʌ/ 'cut'. Depending upon the area of interference from the mother tongue, select words which will be known to the learners and which are easily recognised. Magazines will provide resource materials and the pictures should be mounted on card.

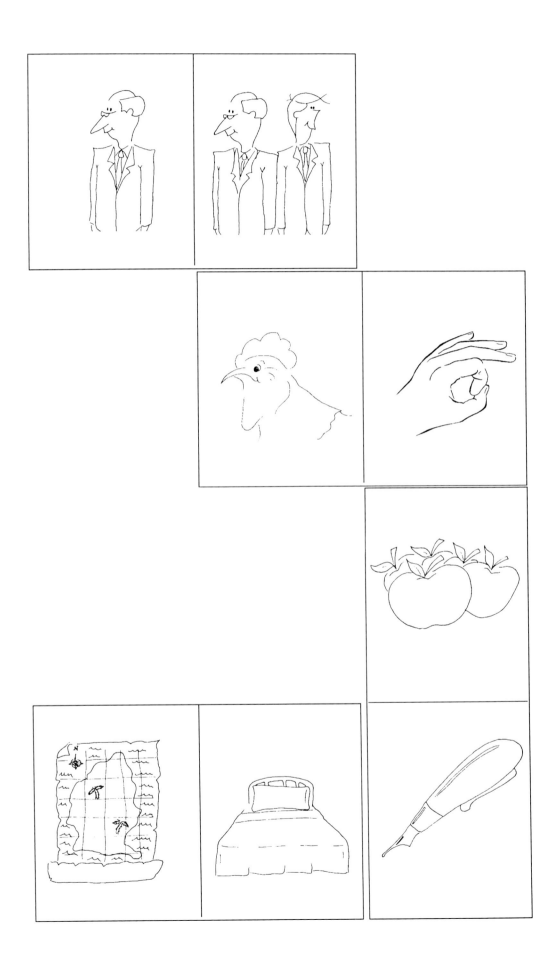

Activity 9: Word Stress

Level: Upper–intermediate.

Methodology: Recognition of stress-placement in the word is important for its correct identification. Word stress should be taught alongside vocabulary building. It is helpful for more advanced learners to work on awareness-arousing tasks to recycle and extend their understanding of this phonological feature.

Materials: Pages from the current course-book (sample p 151)

The teacher selects a page or pages from the learner's current text book and writes up a number of items of vocabulary on the black-board. In the case of 'Aesop' suitable lexis might be

politics	familiar	society
contain	education	entertain

She explains that an important clue to our identification of a polysyllabic word is through correct recognition of the position of the word stress. Word stress is usually fixed within a word but placement does not depend upon meaning. There are some helpful rules for word stress in Rogerson and Gilbert (1990) but this present task is simply to arouse awareness and extend the material in the course book.

Sample words are written on the blackboard and word-families are discussed:

NOUN	ADJECTIVE	VERB
'politics	po'litical	po'liticise
poli'tician		
'family	fa'miliar	fa'miliarise

Learners work individually or in pairs, to look up the word-families of the other lexical items in the text, in their dictionaries.

Awareness-arousing is a good starting point but learning needs to be meaningful and contextualised. In order to help pupils to use their learning in an authentic situation, a field of vocabulary can be examined from the point of view of stress-placement. For example with senior school learners, university subjects might be an appropriate area of interest. Word-patterns can be put up on the blackboard:

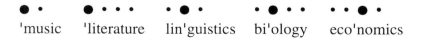

'music   'literature   lin'guistics   bi'ology   eco'nomics

and learners asked to fit the following words under their correct patterns:-

sociology	computing	engineering
politics	mathematics	science
psychology	chemistry	history
medicine	philosophy	geography

Group work

As a skill-using task, pupils can discuss the subject they would most like to study at University or College level and the profession it might lead them into.

Comprehension

Aesop the Storyteller

A fable is a story which teaches a lesson. Fables **contain** important truths about the way people behave to one another as well as providing good entertainment. Many **familiar** sayings in our language **originate** from fables – 'To cry wolf,' for example, or 'One man's meat is another man's poison.'

Perhaps the most famous writer of fables is a man who was called Aesop. He lived about 600 BC and it is believed that he was a slave who was brought to Greece from Africa. The Greeks called him Ethiop, or Aesop. Although he had little **education**, he was a wise man. He knew a lot about people and how they behaved. In Greece, he had a chance to listen to many scholars who discussed the **politics** and **society** of their day. Soon he began to tell stories. Instead of people, he invented animals who spoke and acted much like the Greeks themselves.

Aesop's master was proud of him and enjoyed listening to the inventive stories. He introduced his slave to important people in Greece, and everyone listened to the fables and talked about the morals at the end. Aesop's fame spread throughout the country and he was made a free man. Although some of the fables **contained** harsh comments on Greek society, they encouraged people to reflect upon their attitudes and morals.

Activity 10: Attitudinal Functions of Intonation

Level: Advanced.

Methodology: A role-play for five people.

Materials: Role-play cards for individual members of the group.

Role-plays provide excellent contexts for generating language but they must be well-prepared in advance to ensure success. Items of appropriate vocabulary (and politeness phrases) should be pretaught.

The teacher sets the scene which is a doctor's waiting room. She describes Dr Cameron and several people who have come to consult him. She tells the learners that they must try to sound 'nervous and worried' if they are playing Mr Tweedie or 'complaining' and 'rude' if they are Mrs Cratchet. The class discusses how to sound interested, including extra-linguistic gestures, facial expressions for additional reinforcement of meaning.

 + raised eyebrows + wide pitch!

 + frown and low pitch + doubtful pitch movements.

Group Work

In groups of five, learners are given a character. Each person must think of three adjectives to describe the way their character is feeling. They must tell each other the reason for their visit to Dr Cameron's surgery.

Using the phrases and vocabulary already pretaught, the groups should act out the scene. If possible, the performances should be recorded so that they can be played back and evaluated after the event. The teacher should elicit as much as she can from the learners and establish a simple framework for description using popular terminology such as:

'a happy high voice' or
'a low disappointed voice'.

Part of the learning experience should be to unravel impressions and to link them in to the way in which the characters manipulate the spoken medium.

Scenario

Dr Cameron's Surgery

Dr Cameron is about to start his morning surgery. He is always kind, polite and understanding even when his patients are bad-tempered and rude.

The patients waiting to see him are:

(a) **Mrs Cratchet**
An elderly lady who has broken her ankle and feels very sorry for herself. She is depressed because she can't get out to the shops or visit friends.
(COMPLAINING / RUDE).

(b) **Billy Bilbow**
A ten year old boy who is crying because he has a pain in his stomach. He ate too many crisps and sweets, but doesn't want to tell this to the doctor unless pressed.
(TEARFUL / RELUCTANT)

(c) **Mr Tweedie**
A young man who is very nervous and worried about his cough. He is a car salesman and thinks he might lose his job.
(NERVOUS / WORRIED)

(d) **Mrs Cherry**
A young woman who looks perfectly well and happy. She has just been told she is going to have a baby and is delighted.
(EXCITED / ENTHUSIASTIC).

Role-playing cards on the following page may be photocopied and enlarged for classroom practice.

GLOSSARY

air stream	An airstream is a moving column of air used in the production of speech-sounds. Most speech is produced on the pulmonic egressive airstream initiated from the lungs.
articulators	These are the parts of the vocal tract used to produce speech sounds. The passive articulators, such as the hard palate and the tooth-ridge, are located across the roof of the mouth and the active articulators, such as the lower lip and tongue tip, are located along the base of the mouth. In the production of / f /, the passive articulator is the upper teeth and the active articulator is the lower lip.
assimilation	This refers to the replacement of one phoneme by another under the influence of the phonetic context. *Example:* 'does she?' / ˈdʌʃɪ /; 'Edinburgh' / ˈedɪmˌbərə / ⟵ ⟵
close	Close vowels are produced with the highest point of the tongue close to the roof of the mouth. *Example:* / iː / in 'key', / uː / in 'coo'
consonant	A speech-sound produced with some restriction on the airstream mechanism. *Example:* / p /; / f /
consonant cluster	A group of consonants occuring together with no intervening vowel. *Example:* <u>st</u>a<u>mps</u>
content words	Information-bearing lexical items such as nouns and adjectives.
contractions	The contracted form of auxiliary verbs usual in spoken English. *Example:* I'm, we're
diphthong	A vowel guide which changes in quality during its production. *Example:* / eɪ /, /eə /
discourse	The coherent sequence of ideas or propositions as expressed in language.
elision	The omission of a phoneme or a syllable during connected speech. *Example:* 'next' / neks /; 'Wednesday' / wenzdɪ /

foot	The unit of rhythm similar to a bar in music. The foot begins with a stressed syllable and contains all the following weak syllables up to the next stress.
	Example: / This is the / father of the / bride
	foot foot foot
intonation	Changes affecting pitch patterns in the language, sometimes compared to the melody. See under **thought groups**, **pitch movements**, **main focus** and **key**—all of which go to make up the intonational structuring in the language.
key	Relative pitch height used meaningfully in the language. Neutral or expected key will be mid with movements up to high or down to low providing additional information related to speaker's meaning.
low-termination	The use of low-key at the end of a pitch sequence to denote the end of a turn.
manner of articulation	The way in which the airstream is restricted on its passage up from the lungs.
	Example: stopped / p /, / g / or nasalised /m /, /n/)
main focus	Sometimes referred to as **main sentence stress** or **tonic placement** (Halliday). The speaker tells his listener which is the most crucial word for correct interpretation of the message by pinpointing the stressed syllable in the most important item for main focus. This involves main pitch change, increased vowel length and extra loudness. Items may carry major or minor focus in the thought group. Choice depends on meaning.
monophthong	A pure vowel of unchanging quality. Monophthongs may be long (/ɑː/ in 'c<u>ar</u>', /uː/ in 'sh<u>oe</u>') or short (/e/ in 'r<u>e</u>d', /æ/ in 'm<u>a</u>n').
open	Open vowels are produced with the highest point of the tongue low in the mouth.
	Example: /ɑː/ in 'c<u>ar</u>'
phoneme	A phoneme is the smallest distinctive unit of sound. If the phoneme changes, the meaning must also change.
	Example: <u>f</u>an / <u>v</u>an, h<u>a</u>t / h<u>u</u>t
phonetics	The science of analysing speech production and the description of human speech sounds.
phonology	The study of the sound system of a particular language.

pitch	Pitch is determined by the frequency of vibration of the vocal cords.
pitch movements (or tones)	Changes in pitch direction are used significantly in English to differentiate between grammatical functions (such as statement/question) and to give clues about speaker's attitude (enthusiasm/doubt).
pitch range	During speech, the voice moves up and down between high and low pitch within a scale in which the speaker feels comfortable. This scale, or band, (high → mid → low) is referred to as that speaker's pitch range.
places of articulation	The points along the vocal tract where the airstream is restricted to produce the consonants. *Example:* labial, palatal
proclaiming tones	Falling pitch movements used to convey new information to the listener. Proclaiming tones may be ordinary falls for neutral statement of fact or rise-falls to add extra enthusiasm or commitment (p and p+).
prominence	A term used by Halliday and others to refer to items carrying major and minor focus. *Example:* This is the FATHER of the BRIDE. minor focus MAJOR FOCUS
referring tones	A discourse analyst's term for pitch movements used to signify shared (or referred) information. Referring tones, like proclaiming tones (see above) may be neutral fall-rises (r) or emphatic high rises (r+).
rhythm	The beat in languages is carried either by the ordinary syllable (syllable-timed languages) or the stressed syllable (stress-timed languages). French belongs to the former group and English to the latter.
'Schwa' vowel	The weakened central vowel which only occurs in an unstressed syllable either in the word /ə'weə/ 'a'ware' or in the utterance /ənd ə'nʌðə/ 'and another'.
stress	Relate the occurrence of stress to the syllable-producing mechanism on the airstream. A syllable may be produced either with an ordinary pulse of air (a weak syllable) or a reinforced chest pulse (a stressed syllable).

structural items (or **grammatical words**):	These refer to the low-information items in connected speech such as the articles, the prepositions and the conjunctions. The usual version is the weak form to allow greater highlighting on the content words: *Example:* ~~she~~ arrives ~~on the~~ first ~~of the~~ month / ʃɪ ə/raɪvz n ðə / fɜːst əv ðə / mʌnθ / However, strong forms are found sentence-finally or for special emphasis.
syllable	A central unit for description of phonology. The syllable is one pulse of air (a chest pulse) and may be stressed or weak (see above). The syllable is made up of one or more phonemes and syllables run together to make up the unit of rhythm, the foot.

syllable structure	The make-up of the syllable. This may be:
	
	    cv consonant and vowel see /siː/
	    vc vowel and consonant art / ɑːt /
	
	or complicated clusters:
	
	    ccvcc stamp /stæmp /
	    ccvccc stamps / stæmps /
	
	The formula for syllable-structure in English is:
	
	    C V C
	    0-3 0-4

thought group (or **sense group**)	This is the unit of intonation and it carries a basic pitch pattern. The main pitch movement or pitch change starts on the item of main focus and continues to the end of the group. Thought groups are usually delimited by double slashes // //.
	
	Example: //This is the / <u>father</u> of the / bride //
	        (a falling pitch located on 'father').
	
	The thought-group is made up of one or more feet, just as the foot is made up of one or more syllables and the syllable is made up of one or more phonemes
	
	Example: phoneme /ð/
	                syllable /ðə /
	                foot /fɑːðər əv ðə/
	                thought group //ðɪs ɪz ðə / fɑːðər əv ðə / braɪd//
	
	The thought group is usually regarded as the largest unit in the phonological hierarchy although some authorities such as Brown and Yule (1983) argue that thought groups cluster together to make pitch sequences, or paratones, which structure the spoken language in the same way as paragraphs structure groups of sentences in the written form.

tone   See **pitch movements**. Tone unit - see **thought group**. Tonic syllable - see **main focus**.

utterance   A piece of conversation which frequently corresponds to a sentence.

voicing   States of the vocal cords. If open, the resulting sound is **voiceless** (p, t, s, f); if in vibration the resulting sound is **voiced** (b, d, z, v). Other states of the vocal cords include whispery voice, creaky voice and, if a complete closure is involved, the glottal stop.

vowel   A speech sound produced with open articulation and little restriction of the airstream. Vowel qualities are produced by changes in the shape of the oral cavity and are described with respect to the highest point of the tongue and the lip positions. Vowels may be pure vowels (monophthongs) or changing vowels (diphthongs).

BIBLIOGRAPHY

Abercrombie, D. *Elements of General Phonetics.* Edinburgh University Press. 1964.

Bolinger, D. (ed). *Intonation – Selected Readings.* Penguin Books. 1972.

Bradford, B. *Intonation in Context.* Cambridge University Press. 1988.

Brazil, D. "Phonology. Intonation in Discourse". in T. Van Dÿk (ed) *Handbook of Discourse Analysis.* Academic Press. 1985.

Brazil, D. *Pronunciation for Advanced Learners of English.* Cambridge University Press. 1994.

Brazil, D., Coulthard, M. and Johns, C. *Discourse Intonation and Language Teaching.* Longman. 1981.

Brown, A. (ed). *Teaching English Pronunciation. A Book of Readings.* Routledge. 1991.

Brown, G. *Listening to Spoken English.* Longman. 1977.

Brown, G. and Yule, G. *Teaching the Spoken Language.* Cambridge University Press. 1983.

Brown, G. and Yule, G. *Discourse Analysis.* Cambridge University Press. 1983.

Coulthard, M. *An Introduction to Discourse Analysis.* Longman. 1985.

Dalton, C. and Seidlhofer, B. *Pronunciation.* Oxford University Press. 1995.

Gilbert, J. *Clear Speech.* Cambridge University Press. 1982.

Gumperz, J. *Discourse Strategies.* Cambridge University Press. 1982.

Halliday, M. *A Course in Spoken English.* Oxford University Press. 1970.

Kenworthy, J. *Teaching English Pronunciation.* Longman. 1987.

McCarthy, M. *Discourse Analysis for Language Teachers.* Cambridge University Press. 1991.

Mortimer, C. *Elements of Pronunciation.* Cambridge University Press. 1985.

Nainan, N. *Language Teachers.* Cambridge University Press. 1991.

Roach, P. *English Phonetics and Phonology.* Cambridge University Press. 1983.

Rogerson, P. and Gilbert, J. *Speaking Clearly.* Cambridge University Press. 1990.

Swan, M. and Smith B. *Learner English.* Cambridge University Press. 1987.

Taylor, D. "Non-native Speakers and the Rhythm of English" in *Intenational Review of Applied Linguistics,* 19, 1981.

Taylor, L. *Pronunciation in Action.* Prentice Hall. 1993.

Vaughan Rees, M. "Priorities in Pronunciation Teaching" in *Practical English Teaching,* December 1990 and March 1991.